ONE FOR ALL OLYMPIADS
PREVIOUS YEARS' SOLVED PAPERS
CLASS 1
GENERAL KNOWLEDGE

One Package for All Olympiad Exams

Covers Syllabus of CBSE, CISCE, State Boards & International Boards

- Previous Years' Questions 2011-2019
- SMART BOOK — ACADEMICS' CHOICE AWARD WINNER
- MOST TRUSTED BRANDS OF INDIA 2021
- 3 Levels of Questions: Level 1, 2 & Achievers
- Sample Question Paper for level 1 & 2
- Answer Key-with Explanations
- Chapterwise Mind Maps
- Blended Learning with Print + Online Support

 **1st EDITION** **YEAR 2021-22**

 978-93-5423-337-1

 **Covers Syllabus of CBSE, CISCE, State Board & International Boards**

COPYRIGHT RESERVED BY THE PUBLISHERS

All rights reserved. No part of this book may be reproduced, stored in a retrieval system, or transmitted, in any form or by any means, without written permission from the publishers. The author and publisher will gladly receive information enabling them to rectify any error or omission in subsequent editions.

PUBLISHED BY

 **OSWAAL BOOKS & LEARNING PVT. LTD.**

1/11, Sahitya Kunj, M.G. Road, Agra - 282002, (UP) India

1/1, Cambourne Business Centre Cambridge, Cambridgeshire CB 236DP, United kingdom

0562-2857671
0562-2527781

contact@oswaalbooks.com

www.OswaalBooks.com

DISCLAIMER

Oswaal Books has exercised due care and caution in collecting all the data before publishing this book.
In spite of this, if any omission, inaccuracy or printing error occurs with regard to the data contained in this book, Oswaal Books will not be held responsible or liable.
Oswaal Books will be grateful if you could point out any such error or offer your suggestions which will be of great help for other readers.

Printed at Upkar Printing Unit, Agra

TABLE OF CONTENTS

- Latest Syllabus for Academic year 2020-21 .... 7 - 7

1.	Me and Others in My World	9 - 36
2.	Plants and Animals	37 - 57
3.	Earth and Its Environment	58 - 73
4.	Our Country and the World	74 - 99
5.	Science and Technology	100 - 117
6.	Sports and Entertainment	118 - 136
7.	Language and Literature	137 - 152
8.	Numbers' Magic	153 - 170
9.	Life Skills	171 - 186
10.	Current Affairs	187 - 204
•	Sample Question Paper for Level-1	205 - 212
•	Sample Question Paper for Level-2	213 - 223

HOW TO IMPROVE YOUR CHILD'S GENERAL KNOWLEDGE?

Developing General Knowledge right from the start helps a child stand out in social circles. Feed your child's curiosity and nurture their inquisitive side. Here are some ways to do so.

1. Newspaper headlines

Even adults don't read the whole newspaper, so expecting it from a child is impractical. But reading just the headlines will also familiarise a child with the local and international happenings.

2. Consume better content

Why let your child spend hours watching just cartoons when there are more exciting things to watch? Plan their 'TV time' to include channels like Discovery Channel and National Geographic.

3. Visit the museum

Not every weekend has to be spent at the mall. Plan a trip to the museum or a Science City and watch your child's eyes widen in amazement.

4. Subscribe to News apps

Nowadays it's almost impossible to keep a child away from mobile games. Instead, you can fill the device with applications that give instant notifications for trending news.

LET THE FUN RIDE BEGIN!

Want to make your child future ready?

Olympiad exams can be considered a special avenue of personal growth in a student's life. Children in India get the opportunity to sit for these unique exams every year from a very early age. Olympiads allow parents to understand their child's potential as compared to lakhs of students from all over the country, or even all over the globe. Olympiads test logical thinking and scientific reasoning. They demand a deeper understanding of concepts and help sharpen analytical skills. They nurture curiosity and push students to go the extra mile. Studying diligently for Olympiads is bound to improve a student's grades in school as well. Moreover, these exams train students for other future competitive exams and boost their confidence.

Our Heartfelt Gratitude!

We have taken due care in developing this book. There have been a lot of people who have helped us in our journey. We would like to offer heartfelt gratitude to them- our authors, editors, reviewers.

Classroom is like a pond in which children learn to swim. But one day they will outgrow this pond and will have to swim in the ocean – the real world.

As parents you have the onus of preparing them for this real world. Gone are the days when a child's knowledge or intelligence was judged by their scores in classroom tests. The motive behind Olympiads is to prepare the children for the competition they will be facing beyond the four walls of the classrooms. Olympiads test children's logical and reasoning abilities – two of the most vital and helpful life skills.

Oswaal Books has carefully designed this special edition; Olympiad Previous 10 Years' Solved Papers. The book aims to bring out the best in a child by honing their concepts and sharpening their minds. The book covers syllabi of all leading boards like CBSE, CISCE, State & International Boards.

Learning beyond the regular!

What's so unique about Oswaal One for All Olympiads?

(1) **100% Updated:** Based on the latest exam pattern issued by: UIEO, IEO, IOEL, ISFO, IMO, ISO

(2) **Thorough Practice:** Solved Previous Years' Papers from 2011 to 2020

(3) **Competency Evaluation:** Better assessment through 3 Levels of Questions: Level 1, Level (2 & Achievers

(4) **Valuable Insights:** Find Amazing Facts, Fun Trivia & Did You Know, inside

(5) **Revise & Remember:** Complete concept review with examples

This book aims to make the children exam-ready, boost their confidence and improve their problem-solving ability. With the moto of 'Learning Made Simple', Oswaal Books is constantly striving to make learning simple & accessible for students across the globe.

With Best Wishes!
Team Oswaal Books

SIMPLIFYING YOUR NAVIGATION FOR BETTER USABILITY

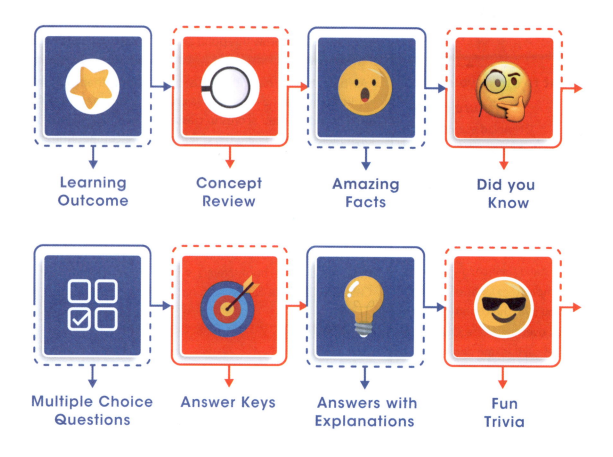

Where to report any plausible content or technical error?

Write to us on: contact@OswaalBooks.com

- Full name of the book with its ISBN
- Mention the page number and specify the error
- You may also upload an image with the error marked, with a little detail of the error.

SYLLABUS

Latest Syllabus for Academic Year (2021-22)

There are so many platforms based on National and International level who are conducting **OLYMPIAD** Exams from class 1 to 12.

Students are able to face the Most Popular below listed exam;

- International Maths Olympiad (IMO)
- Maths Olympiad (ISO)
- Unified International Mathematics Olympiad (UIMO)
- Southeast Asian Mathematical Olympiad (SEAMO)
- International Olympiad of Science (IOS)
- National Level Science Talent Search Examination (NSTSE)
- National Science Olympiad (NSO)
- Science Olympiad (ISO)
- International General Knowledge Olympiad (IGKO)
- International Reasoning & Aptitude Olympiad (IRAO)
- International Talent Hunt Olympiad (ITHO)
- International English Olympiad (IEO)
- Unified International English Olympiad (UIEO)
- International English Language Olympiad (IOEL)
- International Society for Olympiad (ISO)

Since in the race of Olympiad Exam, students are participating from India and Abroad via different channels, so we Oswaal has published a unique book for these exams wherein we have covered the latest syllabus of CBSE, CISCE, IGCSE, IB, and All Indian and International recognised Boards.

Based on the above Boards Curriculum, we have extracted & refined below syllabus:

Syllabus : General Knowledge

Me and My Surroundings, Plants and Animals, India and the World, Science and Technology, Language and Literature, Entertainment, Sports, Maths Fun, Life Skills (Kindness, Soft Skills, Social Skills, Do's & Don'ts), Current Affairs.

Achievers Section: Higher Order Thinking Questions – from the above given Syllabus.

MIND MAPS
Learning Made Simple

When? anytime, as frequency as you like till it becomes a habit!

Why?
- To Unlock the imagination and come up with ideas
- To Remember facts and figures easily
- To Make clearer and better notes
- To Concentrate and save time
- To Plan with ease and ace exams

MIND MAP
AN INTERACTIVE MAGICAL TOOL

What? presenting words and concepts as pictures!!

Result Learning made simple 'a winning combination'

How? With a blank sheet of paper coloured pens and your creative imagination!

DECODING A MIND MAP

➤ **First Associations**   ～ **Second Associations**   ⤴ **Third Associations**

The arrows used in the Mind Maps point to different Levels of Associations. Associations spreading out straight from the core concept are the First Level of Association. Then we have a Second Level of Association emitting from the first level and the chronology continues.

(8)

Me and Others in My World

CHAPTER 1
ME AND OTHERS IN MY WORLD

Learning Outcomes

About Me
Children would be able to:
- Share and verbally communicate their personal details;
- Identify and name the parts of the body;
- Distinguish between functions of different parts of the body;
- Share their hobbies, likes and dislikes and learn to appreciate those of others;
- Cite examples of food items received from plants and animals;
- Distinguish between various kinds of houses seen in the surroundings;
- Understanding the need and importance of clothing for human beings;
- Identify the kinds of clothes/ dresses worn by them and their family members.

Others in My World
- Name the family members verbally;
- Identify and differentiate between a Joint and a Nuclear Family;
- Identify relationships between different family members;
- Describe the family's role and responsibilities in his/ her own words;
- Appreciate the need for neighbours (society) and friends;
- Identify various places, like, school, hospital, park, water bodies, etc., in the neighbourhood;
- Discuss the roles played by various people in these places.

Concept Review

INTRODUCTION

It is a natural phenomenon that as a child grows up, he becomes curious about the environment around him. In this way, this chapter is all about making children aware of themselves and others in their world.

Me and Others in My World

 **About Me**

PERSONAL DETAILS

★ **Personal Details Include:**

1. Name
2. Name of parents
3. Name of the siblings(if any)
4. Address
5. Birthday
6. Phone/ Mobile number

★ **Human Body Parts:**

- Our body is amazing! We do all the work with our body. It is our thinking and reasoning ability that makes us unique among all living creatures on the Earth. Our ability to communicate makes us human.

- Our body is made up of many parts, each has its own unique function. Let us know the names of the parts of our body:

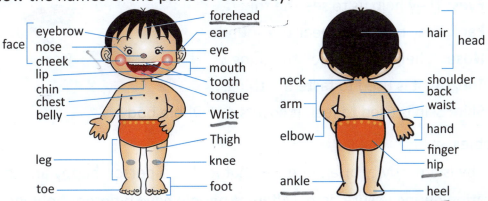

Parts of the Body

1. **Head:** The head is one of the most important parts of the body. The head protects the brain, which is responsible for all the functions of our body. Our head is full of hair. The front side of the head is the face with the forehead, eyes, nose, mouth, cheek, chin, etc. Teeth are present inside our mouth, which are used to bite and chew the food. Below the head is the neck.

2. **Chest:** Below the neck is our chest. Underneath the chest, there is a heart that beats continuously. Lungs are also present in the chest. Human body has two lungs. The shoulder lies between the neck and the chest, where the arms are connected. Belly is just below the chest.

DID YOU KNOW?

- Babies are born with 300 bones – However, an adult has 206 bones.
- Your lungs are the only organs in your body that float.
- Your eyeballs are actually part of your brain.

3. **Arms:** Shoulders are joined to arms. There are two arms -- the right arm and the left arm. The elbow is a joint present in the middle of the upper and lower arm. At the end of the arm, there is a hand consisting of four fingers and one thumb.

4. **Legs:** Below the belly are the legs. The upper part of the leg is called thigh. Below the thigh is the knee which is also a joint like elbow. Below the knee are the calves that are present on the back side of the lower leg. The bottommost part of the lower leg is the foot. Each foot has five toes. Ankle is the joint connecting the foot and the lower leg.

★ **Sense Organs**

Sense organs are special organs that help us to become aware of the world around us. There are five sense organs as given below:

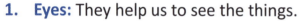

Sense Organs

Eye Nose Ear

Tongue Skin

1. **Eyes:** They help us to see the things.
2. **Ears:** They help us to hear the sounds.
3. **Nose:** It helps us to smell the things.
4. **Tongue:** It is used to taste the things.
5. **Skin:** Skin is used to feel. It covers our whole body.

★ **Hobbies**

A hobby is an activity or an interest that makes a person happy and is done for relaxation during leisure time. Different people have different hobbies. Some of them are:

1. Reading books
2. Playing different types of indoor games
3. Playing different types of outdoor games
4. Watching cartoon
5. Dancing
6. Singing
7. Cooking
8. Photography
9. Gardening
10. Playing musical instruments

AMAZING FACTS

- While you are sleeping, you can't smell anything – not even really, bad or potent smells.
- Girls have more taste buds than boys.

Me and Others in My World

Fishing   Swimming   Cooking

Horse riding   Skateboarding   Cycling

Doing exercises   Rafting   Dancing

Painting   Hiking   Camping

★ **Likes and Dislikes**

- Likes are something which we love and dislikes which we don't love. Factors that influence our likes and dislikes include family background, occupation, traditions, mental state, etc.

DID YOU KNOW?

Apple sauce was the first food eaten in space by astronauts.

13

 My Needs

Human being are dependent on few basic needs for living, without which they cannot survive. These needs are food, shelter and clothes.

DID YOU KNOW?

February is the National Hot Breakfast Month.

★ **Food**

- Food is our basic necessity and is important to live. Food gives us energy to work.
- There are many kinds of food that we get from plants and animals like:

1. **Fruits and Vegetables:** Important for preventing different diseases.
2. **Grains:** Give energy to work, play, learn and for other activities.
3. **Milk and Milk Products:** Keep our bones strong and healthy.
4. **Egg, Meat and Fish:** Important for muscle growth.

Food from Plants	Food from Animals
We get most of our food from plants. The food which we get from plants are called Vegetarian food.	We also get many food item from animals. Most of the food which we get from animals are called Non-Vegetarian food.

Me and Others in My World

★ **In a day, a person must have the following meals:**
1. **Breakfast:** People eat breakfast early in the morning. It is very important as it breaks the overnight fasting period and provides energy and required nutrients to the body.
2. **Lunch:** People have lunch in the afternoon. It includes proper meals and helps people to grow and stay healthy.
3. **Dinner:** It is the meal that people have in the evening.

★ **Healthy Eating Habits**
1. Eat fresh food.
2. Don't talk or make noise while eating.
3. Chew the food properly.
4. Take only as much food as you could eat in plate.
5. Don't spill food on the table or on clothes.
6. Eat healthy food.
7. Drink at least 6 to 8 glasses of water every day.

★ **Shelter**
- Shelter protects human beings from cold, rain, Sun, wild animals, etc.
- We can find various types of houses around us. Some of them are:

1. **Kutcha House:** It is made up of mud, bamboo, wood, straw, etc., and is usually found in small towns and villages.

AMAZING FACT

Many people around the world live in caves even today.

2. **Pucca House:** It is made up of cement, iron, bricks, wood, etc. and usually found in big towns and cities. It is also called permanent house. Nowadays, we can see big multi-storied buildings having many apartments or flats.

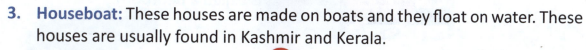

3. **Houseboat:** These houses are made on boats and they float on water. These houses are usually found in Kashmir and Kerala.

4. **Caravan:** It is a kind of temporary house, made on wheels. It is also known as 'House on Wheels' and can move from one place to another.

5. **Igloo:** Igloos are made up of snow and found in very cold regions. It is also known as 'Snow House'. People living in igloos are known as Eskimos.

AMAZING FACTS

You can build fire inside igloo. It just needs to be in the centre of the igloo so that it is farthest from the walls and a hole is needed on the top of the igloo, to allow the smoke to escape.

6. **Tent:** House made up of strong cloth is known as Tent. These houses are made by scouts, soldiers, nomads, people who usually go for camping, etc. It is a kind of temporary house.

★ **Different Rooms in a House**

A house has many rooms and we use each room for a different purpose.

A room where we spend time with family, sit and talk with our guests is called a **living room**.

A room where we sleep and take rest is called a **bedroom**.

Me and Others in My World

Dining room is a room where we eat food with our family.

Food is cooked in the **kitchen**.

Bathroom is used to take bath and clean ourselves.

Storeroom is used to store the things.

We do a lot of things in our house such as work, cook, eat, sleep, spend our time, etc. Thus, we should keep our house clean and tidy. We should also clean and decorate our house during festivals with lights, candles, flowers, rangoli, paintings, flower pots, etc.

★ **Clothing**

Clothes protect us from heat, rain, cold, Sun, wind, insect bites, dust and dirt. We wear different clothes according to the weather:

1. We wear cotton clothes in summer to keep us cool.
2. We wear woollen clothes in winter to keep us warm.
3. We wear raincoats in monsoon season to protect us from getting wet.

Summer   Winter   Monsoon

DID YOU KNOW?

Cotton and linen fabrics are made from plants, while silk fabric is made from fibers spun by the silkworms.

4. People also wear clothes according to their region.

Maharashtrian dress **Bengali Dress** **Gujarati dress**

> **FUN TRIVIA**
> High heels shoes were came into fashion and first intended for men in the 10th century.

5. We wear standard set of clothing for school. This is called a school uniform. Different schools have different school uniforms.

> **DID YOU KNOW?**
> In other countries sometimes men also wear skirts such as togas and kilts.

 My Family

★ **Family**

- People who live together with marriage bonds, blood relations or adoption bonds, as a unit form a family.

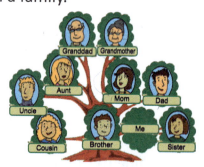

1. **Big Family/Joint Family:** A family which is large in size with three or more generations such as grandparents, parents, brothers, sisters, uncles, aunts and cousins living in the same home is called a Big Family.

Joint Family

Me and Others in My World

2. **Small Family/Nuclear Family:** A family consisting of only parents (mother and father) and their children is called a Small Family or Nuclear Family.

Nuclear Family

★ **Why is Family Important?**

Family is the most important thing in our life and each family member has a different role such as:

1. Family members provide love, advice, support and protection to each other.
2. Family members help to develop sense of self-confidence and self-esteem.
3. Family members provide a sense of belongingness.

★ **How are Families Different**

Each family differs from another in terms of religion, cultures, habits, language, size of families, etc. For example:

1. A family may follow Hinduism, Islam, Christianity, etc.
2. A family may speak English, Hindi, Punjabi, etc.
3. A family may have different food habits.
4. A family may be a joint family or a nuclear family.

★ **Loving, Caring and Sharing**

- In a family, each member cares for the other and participates in the housework. Grandparents share the responsibility in the form of buying vegetables from market, gardening, taking children to the park for a walk or for playing teaching good habits to the children, telling moral stories at bedtime to the children, etc. In this way, they also share household responsibilities.

- Mother cooks for everyone and does most of the housework. She takes care of the children and other family members when they are sick and also takes care of everyone in the family.

- Father goes to the office and supports the family financially. He also helps others to do household chores.

- An elder brother or sister helps his/her younger brother or sister to finish their homework, keep their toys safely after playing, takes care of the elderly in the family and helps in doing household chores.

- Younger ones help by keeping their room neat and clean. They also help the elder members by sharing their responsibilities, e.g., helping grandparents in gardening, helping mother in certain other household works.

Me and Others in My World

 My Surroundings

★ **My Friends**

Friends also play an important role in our life. They care about us. We share our joys, sorrows, ideas, toys, etc., with our friends. We also play and enjoy with our friends.

★ **Community Helpers**

Community helpers are those people who help us everyday as a part of their job.

1. **Postman** delivers letters and telegrams.
2. **Farmer** works in the field and grows crops, grains, fruits, vegetables, etc. for us.
3. **Tailor** stitches clothes for us.
4. **Doctor** cures patients.
5. **Nurse** takes care of us when we are sick.
6. **Policeman** protects us and our property from thieves.
7. **Plumber** fits, repairs and maintains water supply system.
8. **Fire fighter** extinguishes fire.
9. **Blacksmith** creates and repairs objects made up of iron.
10. **Carpenter** creates and repairs objects made up of wood.

★ **Neighbourhood**

The surrounding area or region near some place or thing is called neighbourhood.

1. **Park:** A park is an area near a particular region or community having lots of trees and plants. It also has swings, slides and seesaws for children to play there. Elderly and other people go to park for early morning walks or evening walks.

2. **School:** School is known as the second home for children. Children go to school every day. In school, teachers teach them and help them in learning new and good things. Children also make friends in school.

3. **Market:** A market is a place in our neighbourhood where we go to buy things of daily needs such as vegetables, fruits, books, bread, flowers, clothes, etc.

4. **Post Office:** A post office is a place in our neighbourhood where we post letters.

Me and Others in My World

5. **Hospital:** A hospital is a place where people visit when they are sick. It is a place where doctors and nurses work.

6. **Police Station:** Police station is a place where policemen work. They help us by catching and punishing thieves and robbers.

7. **Fire Station:** Fire station is a place where fire fighters. We call the fire station, whenever there is any fire in our neighbourhood.

8. **Railway Station:** Railway station is a place where we go when we want to board a train.

9. **Bus Stop:** Bus stop is a place where people board a bus and get down from the bus.

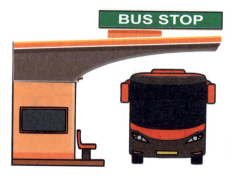

10. **Bank:** Bank is a place where we keep our money. We visit the bank when we want to withdraw or deposit money.

DID YOU KNOW?
Jama Masjid in Delhi in the largest mosque in India.

★ **Places of Worship:** There are many places of worship where people go to pray as per the religion they follow.

Temple

Gurudwara

Church

Mosque

Me and Others in My World

Multiple Choice Questions

LEVEL 1

1. Which of the following fruits you can eat only after peeling?

   (a) 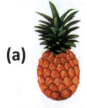 (b)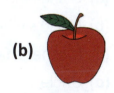

   (c)   (d)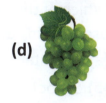

   [2019]

2. Who worship at the place shown in the picture?
   (a) Hindus
   (b) Christians
   (c) Muslims
   (d) Sikhs   [2019]

3. Identify the vegetable shown in the picture.
   (a) Turnip
   (b) Radish
   (c) Cauliflower
   (d) Beetroot   [2019]

4. My father's parents are my _____ grandparents.
   (a) Great
   (b) Paternal
   (c) Maternal
   (d) Both (b) and (c)   [2019]

5. Which of the following is a correct match?
   (a) Head - Glove
   (b) Eyes - Glasses
   (c) Wrist - Shoes
   (d) Neck - Hat   [2018]

6. Choose the word partner of the given word.

   PARKING

   (a) House   (b) Hotel
   (c) Lot   (d) Shop   [2018]

7. The vegetable shown in the picture is _____ .
   (a) Cauliflower
   (b) Cabbage
   (c) Broccoli
   (d) Turnip   [2018]

8. Muslims worship in a _____

   (a)

   (b)

   (c)

(d) **[2018]**

9. Identify the fruit shown in the picture.
   (a) Plum
   (b) Peach
   (c) Litchi
   (d) Cherry **[2018]**

10. The person who teaches us in schools is our _____ .
    (a) Watchman (b) Sweeper
    (c) Teacher (d) None of these **[2017]**

11. He makes sure that we obey the traffic rules.
    (a) Fireman
    (b) Army man
    (c) Traffic policeman
    (d) All of these **[2017]**

12. Which of the following gives us energy to work and play?
    (a)  Rice
    (b)  Vegetables
    (c)  Fruits
    (d) All of these **[2017]**

13. How many glasses of water we should drink daily?
    (a) 6-8 (b) 7-9
    (c) 3-4 (d) 8-10 **[2017]**

14. Which of the following is an INCORRECT match?
    (a) Grandfather's wife → Grandmother
    (b) Uncle's wife → Aunt
    (c) Mother's father → Grandfather
    (d) Uncle's son → Nephew **[2016]**

15. Which of the following places do we use to study and learn?
    (a) Hospital
    (b) School
    (c) Kitchen
    (d) Drawing room **[2016]**

16. Who protects our country from Enemies?
    (a) Fireman
    (b) Army man
    (c) Traffic policeman
    (d) None of these **[2016]**

17. How many teeth are present in an adult?
    (a) 20 (b) 30
    (c) 32 (d) 64 **[2016]**

18. The figure given below shows some parts of a human body.

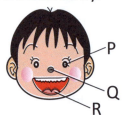

Identify the parts P, Q and R.

	P	Q	R
(a)	Nose	Tongue	Skin
(b)	Eye	Nose	Tongue
(c)	Tongue	Ear	Nose
(d)	Ear	Nose	Eye

[2016]

19. A family that consists of mother, father and children is known as a _____.
    (a) Joint family
    (b) Small family
    (c) Big family
    (d) Good family   [2015]

20. If my family consists of 4 members, in that case the fourth member of my family will be my _____.
    (a) Sister
    (b) Teacher
    (c) Gardener
    (d) All of these   [2015]

21. Which of these is least likely to be found in the kitchen?

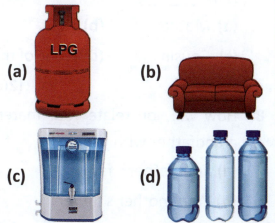

[2015]

22. Who brings letters to your house?
    (a) Teacher
    (b) Nurse
    (c) Postman
    (d) Driver   [2015]

23. Which of the following parts controls all the activities in our body?
    (a) Eyes   (b) Ears
    (c) Brain   (d) Nose   [2015]

24. Rahul is playing video game on television. Which of the following parts of the body is are being used?

   (a) Eye
   (b) Nose
   (c) Ear
   (d) Both (a) and (c)   [2015]

25. Which of the following festivals, are the children celebrating in the given picture?

   (a) Holi
   (b) Diwali
   (c) Christmas
   (d) Eid

LEVEL 2

1. If you want to buy the items given in the box, then where would you go?

Glue, Notebooks, Whiteboard marker, Sharpener

   (a) Grocery store
   (b) Bakery shop
   (c) Stationery shop
   (d) Barber shop [2019]

2. Who among the following uses the tools shown in the box?

Spanner	Hammer	Pliers

   (a) Soldier
   (b) Plumber
   (c) Tailor
   (d) Teacher [2019]

3. My maternal uncle's daughter is Priyanka. How is Priyanka related to me?
   (a) Nephew   (b) Niece
   (c) Cousin   (d) Aunt [2019]

4.

   Mini is talking about _____ .
   (a) Legs   (b) Hands
   (c) Eyes   (d) Ears [2018]

5. The _____ takes care of the school garden.
   (a) Gardener
   (b) Teacher
   (c) Milkman
   (d) All of the above [2017]

6. Match the List I with List II :

	LIST I		LIST II
A.	Kutcha house	1.	Father
B.	Pucca house	2.	Mud
C.	School	3.	Bricks
D.	Family	4.	Teachers

	A	B	C	D
(a)	1	3	4	2
(b)	2	3	4	1
(c)	1	3	4	2
(d)	1	2	3	4

   [2017]

7. Rupa is the sister of my father. Rupa is my _____ .
   (a) Mother   (b) Aunt
   (c) Cousin   (d) None of these [2017]

8. How will you relate your maternal grandfather with yourself?
   (a) Your father's father
   (b) Your mother's father
   (c) Your father's grandfather
   (d) None of these [2016]

Me and Others in My World

9. Which of the following is a family occasion?

(a)

(b)

(c)

(d) Both (b) & (c) [2016]

10. Who among the following persons stitches your clothes?

(a)

(b)

(c)

(d)

[2016]

11. You have to go to your friend's birthday party but you want to change your hairstyle. Who will help you to get a new hairstyle?
(a) Barber (b) Teacher
(c) Tailor (d) Cobbler
[2016]

12. Which of the following is NOT a good habit?

(a)

(b)

(c)

(d)

[2016]

13. Toes and knees are the parts of:
(a) Arms (b) Heart
(c) Lungs (d) Legs [2016]

14. Rahul is the brother of Gitanjali and father of Mayank. What will Mayank call Gitanjali?
(a) Mother (b) Sister
(c) Aunt (d) Sister-in-law
[2016]

15. Who among the following helps you when you have high fever and stomach pain?
    (a) Doctor
    (b) Policeman
    (c) Milkman
    (d) Tailor [2015]

16. Match the Column (I) with Column (II).

COLUMN (I)		COLUMN (II)	
A.	Eyes	1.	Walking
B.	Legs	2.	Loudspeaker
C.	Ears	3.	Ice-cream
D.	Tongue	4.	Television

	A	B	C	D
(a)	4	3	2	1
(b)	3	4	1	2
(c)	4	1	2	3
(d)	2	3	4	1

[2015]

17. Solve the Riddle.
    I catch the thieves and make sure that everybody follow the rules. Who I am?
    (a) Policeman   (b) Carpenter
    (c) Milkman   (d) Doctor
    [2015]

18. Different body parts have different roles. We use 'X' to smell. We also use it to breathe. Which part of the body is 'X'?
    (a) Ear   (b) Nose
    (c) Eye   (d) Mouth

19. With the help of the picture, identify Rahul is _____.
    (a) Happy
    (b) Sad
    (c) Afraid
    (d) Surprised

20. Which of the following we should not wear in winter?

(a)  (b)

(c)   (d)

Me and Others in My World

ACHIEVERS SECTION

1. Match the columns and select the correct option.

COLUMN I		COLUMN II	
A.	Pizza	1.	Potato
B.	Chocolate	2.	Rice
C.	French Fries	3.	Cheese
D.	Poha	4.	Cocoa beans

	A	B	C	D
(a)	4	3	2	1
(b)	1	4	3	2
(c)	2	1	3	4
(d)	3	4	1	2

[2019]

2. Lalita is Kapil's grandmother and Raghav is Kapil's father. Then what is the relationship between Lalita and Raghav?
   (a) Father - Son
   (b) Mother- Son
   (c) Brother - Sister
   (d) Uncle - Neice [2017]

3. Which of the following options replaces 'X' and 'Y' in the following? Match the phrases with the given words.

Healthy Food	Fruits	Vegetables
Junk food	'X'	Chocolates
cotton clothes	Frock	'Y'

   (a) X = Burger, Y = Raincoat
   (b) X = Pizza, Y = Shirt
   (c) X = Fruit, Y = Vegetables
   (d) X = Chocolates, Y = Sweater
   [2017]

4. An organ is a:
   (a) Group of tissues
   (b) Group of cells
   (c) Group of bees
   (d) All of the above [2017]

5. Consider the following two statements:
   Statement A : Husband and wife are not family members.
   Statement B : Cousins are family members of a small family.
   (a) Statement A is correct.
   (b) Statement B is correct.
   (c) Statements A and B are correct.
   (d) Neither Statement A nor Statement B is correct. [2015]

Answer-Key

LEVEL 1

1. (a)	2. (b)	3. (d)	4. (b)	5. (b)
6. (c)	7. (d)	8. (c)	9. (c)	10. (c)
11. (c)	12. (a)	13. (a)	14. (d)	15. (b)
16. (b)	17. (c)	18. (b)	19. (b)	20. (a)
21. (b)	22. (c)	23. (c)	24. (d)	25. (a)

LEVEL 2

1. (c)	2. (b)	3. (c)	4. (a)	5. (a)
6. (b)	7. (b)	8. (b)	9. (d)	10. (b)
11. (a)	12. (b)	13. (d)	14. (c)	15. (a)
16. (c)	17. (a)	18. (b)	19. (b)	20. (d)

ACHIEVERS SECTION

1. (d)	2. (b)	3. (b)	4. (a)	5. (d)

Answers with Explanations

LEVEL 1

1. **Correct option is (a)**
   Explanation: Pineapple has inedible skin as its skin is bumpy and spiny.

2. **Correct option is (b)**
   Explanation: Christians worship in church. Churches have a cross on their steeples or cupolas.

3. **Correct option is (d)**
   Explanation: Beetroot is dark red in color and has a round or cylindrical tapered shape. It has a short tail at the bottom.

4. **Correct option is (b)**
   Explanation: Paternal grandparents are father's parents and maternal grandparents are mother's parents.

5. **Correct option is (b)**
   Explanation: We wear hat on head, glasses on eyes, watch on wrist, and scarf or tie on neck.

Me and Others in My World

8. **Correct option is (c)**
   Explanation: Mosque is Muslims' house of Worship.

10. **Correct option is (c)**
    Explanation: Teacher teaches us in school.

11. **Correct option is (c)**
    Explanation: Traffic policeman directs us as per traffic rules.

12. **Correct option is (a)**
    Explanation: Rice is a cereal and cereals give us energy to play, work, learn, walk, etc.

13. **Correct option is (a)**
    Explanation: Children should drink 6-8 glasses of water daily to avoid dehydration.

14. **Correct option is (d)**
    Explanation: Our uncle's son is our cousin.

15. **Correct option is (b)**
    Explanation: School is a place where we go to study and learn.

16. **Correct option is (b)**
    Explanation: Army man fights for the nation and protects our country from enemies.

17. **Correct option is (c)**
    Explanation: An adult has 32 teeth, 16 in upper jaw and 16 in lower jaw.

18. **Correct option is (b)**
    Explanation: 'P' is representing eye, 'Q' is representing nose and 'R' is representing tongue.

19. **Correct option is (b)**
    Explanation: A family consisting of mother, father and their children is known as small family / nuclear family.

20. **Correct option is (a)**
    Explanation: Teacher and gardener are not family members.

21. **Correct option is (b)**
    Explanation: Sofa is found in the drawing or living room.

22. **Correct option is (c)**
    Explanation: Postman works in post office and brings letters at our door step.

23. **Correct option is (c)**
    Explanation: Brain controls our behavior, thinking and actions.

24. **Correct option is (d)**
    Explanation: Eyes are being used to see the picture on the screen and ears are being used to hear the sound.

25. **Correct option is (a)**
    Explanation: Holi is the festival of colours. In the given picture, children are playing with colours.

Level 2

1. **Correct option is (c)**
   Explanation: We buy grocery items such as cereals, oils, sauces, nuts, snack mixes, etc., from grocery shop. We buy buns, rolls, biscuits, breads, cookies, desserts, baked food etc., from bakery shop. We buy stationery products such as glue, notebook, whiteboard marker, sharpener, etc., from stationery shop. We get services such as cutting, trimming and styling of hair from barber shop.

2. **Correct option is (b)**
   Explanation: Plumber fixes and repairs water supply system using various tools such as hammer, spanner, pliers, etc.

3. **Correct option is (c)**
   Explanation: My maternal uncle will be brother of my mother and his daughter will be my cousin.

4. **Correct option is (a)**
   Explanation: Human beings have two legs which are used to walk and run. Lions have four legs.

5. **Correct option is (a)**
   Explanation: The job of a gardener is to take care of the garden.

6. **Correct option is (b)**
   Explanation: Kutcha house is made up of mud, pucca house is made up of bricks, school is a place where teachers teach us, and father is a family member.

7. **Correct option is (b)**
   Explanation: My father's sister is my aunt.

8. **Correct option is (b)**
   Explanation: Mother's father is maternal grandfather.

9. **Correct option is (d)**
   Explanation: Birthday and marriage, both are family occasions. Diwali is a festival.

10. **Correct option is (b)**
    Explanation: The given options show cobbler, tailor, farmer and architect respectively. Tailor stitches clothes for us.

11. **Correct option is (a)**
    Explanation: Barber trims, cuts, and style our hair.

12. **Correct option is (b)**
    Explanation: Everyone should keep their things in a proper order.

13. **Correct option is (d)**
    Explanation: Toes and Knee are the parts of Legs. Joint present in the middle of leg is Knee and toes are present at the end of human foot.

14. **Correct option is (c)**
    Explanation:
    Mayank, will call her aunt

    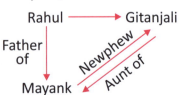

Me and Others in My World

15. Correct option is (a)
   Explanation: People visit a doctor when they are sick.

16. Correct option is (c)
   Explanation: Eyes are used to watch television, legs are used to walk, ears are used to hear the sound of loudspeaker and tongue is used to taste ice-cream.

17. Correct option is (a)
   Explanation: The duty of policeman is to maintain law and order and catch thieves.

18. Correct option is (b)
   Explanation: Nose is a sense organ which is used to breathe and smell.

20. Correct option is (d)
   Explanation: We use raincoat in monsoon or rainy season to avoid getting wet.

ACHIEVERS SECTION

1. Correct option is (d)
   Explanation: Pizza is made up of cheese, chocolate is made up of cocoa beans, french fries is made up of potato, and poha is made up of rice.

2. Correct option is (b)
   Explanation:

   Kapil ←— Grandmother of —— Lalita
   ↑ Father of   ↑ Son of / Mother of
   Raghav

3. Correct option is (b)
   Explanation: Pizza is an example of junk food and shirt is an example of cotton clothing.

4. Correct option is (a)
   Explanation: An organ is a group of tissues with similar functions.

5. Correct option is (d)
   Explanation: Husband and wife are family members.
   Small family consists of mother, father and their children only. Thus, cousins are not family members of a small family.

General Knowledge One For All Olympiads Solved Papers, Class-1

How to make learning
Fun, Effective & Responsive
at the same time?

It's easy!
Scan the QR codes below

Body Parts

Food We Eat

Shelter

and get started!

Plants and Animals

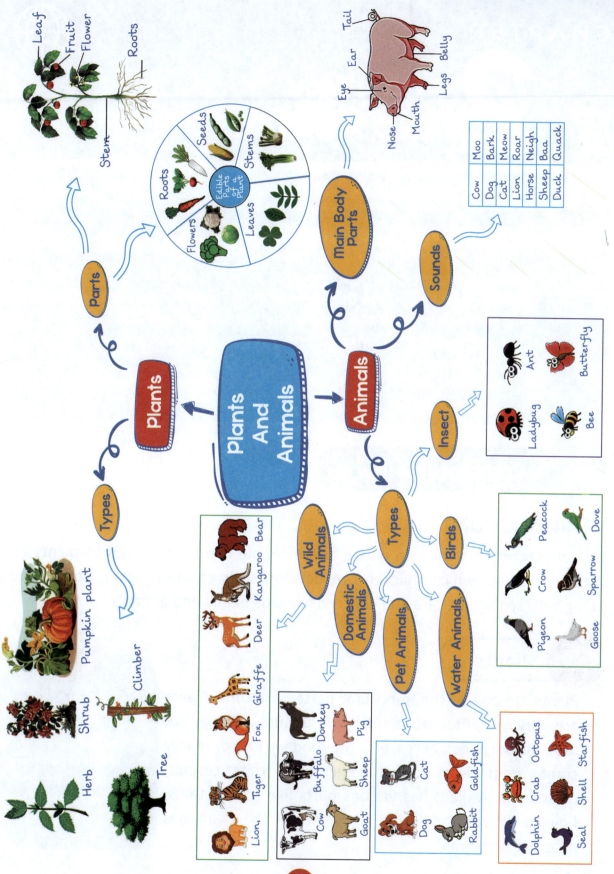

CHAPTER 2
PLANTS AND ANIMALS

Learning Outcomes

Children would be able to:
- ✓ Know about plants and the main parts of a plant;
- ✓ Cite examples of some medicinal plants used at home;
- ✓ Recognize and name the animals/birds seen in the surroundings;
- ✓ Identify and name the main body parts of animals;
- ✓ Identify and differentiate between pet, domestic and wild animals by citing examples;
- ✓ Recognize the sounds made by some common animals and birds and mimic them.

Concept Review

INTRODUCTION

This chapter makes children aware about simple concepts related to plants and animals through which children can develop skills of observation, appreciation along with sensitivity, care and concern towards plants and animals.

Plants

Plants are one of the important parts of nature. Plants are very useful for us as they give us many things like food, wood, paper, herbs, etc. The food we eat, primarily comes from plants such as vegetables, fruits, cereals, pulses, etc. A plant has various parts like roots, stems, flowers, leaves and fruits. Each part of the plant has different functions.

DID YOU KNOW?

Water travels in the upward direction from the roots to its stem and then into the plant leaves.

Plants and Animals

★ **Parts of a Plant:**
1. **Root**
   - It grows below the soil surface.
   - It holds the plant firmly in its place.
   - It provides support to the plant and stores food.
2. **Stem**
   - It is green or brown in colour.
   - It provides support to the whole upper part of the plant.
   - It carries water and other minerals from roots to other parts of the plant.

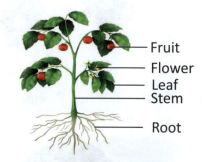

3. **Leaf**
   - It is the green structure of the plant prepares food for the plant.
   - It is attached to the stem/ branch.
   - Leaves of different plants have different shape, size, and colour.

4. **Flower**
   - It is the most attractive and colourful part of the plant.
   - Flowers of different plants have different shape, size, and colour.
   - It changes into fruit.

5. **Fruit**
   - It is the fleshy and ripened part of the plant.
   - It encloses seed or seeds.

★ **Types of Plants**
1. **Herbs:** These plants are small in size and have a soft stem. For example, carrot, radish, coriander, ginger, spinach, mint, etc.

DID YOU KNOW?

Apple's volume consists of 25% air that is why it floats on water.

Mint   Coriander   Spinach

2. **Shrubs:** These are small and bushy plants with hard stem and branches. For example, rose, tulsi, hibiscus, cotton, etc.

Rose plant   Tulsi plant   Hibiscus plant

DID YOU KNOW?
The country Brazil is named after a tree.

3. **Trees:** Trees are big, tall and strong plants. For example, mango, neem, banyan, coconut tree, etc.

Neem tree   Banyan tree   Coconut tree

4. **Climbers:** These are weak plants and they need help of another plant or support to grow upright. For example, grapevine, money plant, pea, Beans, etc.

Grapevine   Pea   Money Plant

5. **Creepers:** These plants grow along the soil. For example, pumpkin, watermelon, muskmelon, gourd, etc.

Pumpkin plant   Watermelon plant   Muskmelon plant

6. **Water Plants (Aquatic Plants):** Water plants grow in water. For example, lotus, water lily, etc.

Lotus

Water lily

7. **Medicinal Plants:** Some plants are used to prepare medicines, for example, tulsi, aloevera, neem, etc.

Neem　　　　Tulsi　　　　Aloevera

AMAZING FACTS
- Banana is actually an Arabic word for fingers.
- Bananas contain a natural chemical that makes people feel happy.
- Apples, onions and potatoes have the same taste. Test this by closing your nose while eating them.

★ **Edible Parts of Plants**

Parts of Plant	Examples
Roots	 Carrot　Beetroot　Radish
Leaves	Cabbage　Spinach
Fruits	Apple　Banana　Pomegranate
Flowers	Cauliflower　Broccoli
Stems	Ginger　Sugarcane

DID YOU KNOW?
A cucumber is not a vegetable. It is a fruit as it has seeds.

★ **Taking Care of Plants**
1. Plant more and more trees.
2. Water them regularly.
3. Add manure to the soil regularly.
4. Don't step on small plants and flower beds.
5. Don't cut down trees or plants.

Animals

In our surrounding, we see various types of animals which differ in size, colour, and shape.

★ **Main Body Parts of Animals**
- Animals mostly have four legs, two eyes, two ears, one nose, one mouth and one tail.

DID YOU KNOW?

Cheetah is the fastest land animal in the world.

★ **Animals in Our Surroundings**
1. **Wild Animals:** Wild animals live in jungle. We can also see wild animals in the zoo. Wild animals are dangerous and fierce.

| Giraffe | Zebra | Monkey | Snake | Crocodile | Deer |

2. **Domestic Animals:** Domestic animals are those animals which live with us.

| Cow | Buffaloe | Goat | Sheep | Ox | Horse |

Plants and Animals

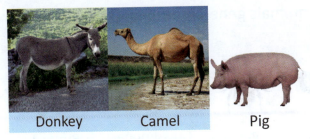

Donkey   Camel   Pig

3. **Pet Animals:** Pet animals are those which live with us in our homes and use love to play with them.

Dog   Cat   Parrot

DID YOU KNOW?
The average life of a dog depending upon the breed can vary from 10 to 14 years.

4. **Reptiles:** Reptiles crawl on the ground. Some of them have short legs while some do not have legs.

Snakes   Tortoise

Lizard   Chameleon   Crocodile

DID YOU KNOW?
Pigeons are believed to be the first bird to deliver messages.

5. **Birds:** Birds are animals with feathers, wings, two legs and a beak. Birds usually fly in the air, but some birds can swim in the water also, for example, duck.

Eagle   Pigeon   Sparrow   Parrot

Peacock   Duck   Hen

FUN TRIVIA
God has have fixed horn on horse and misplaced on its forehead and named it as 'Unicorn'

6. **Insects:** These are small animals generally with six legs and one or two pair of wings.

Cockroach   Housefly   Bee   Grasshopper   Butterfly

7. **Water Animals:** Animals that live in water are known as water animals.

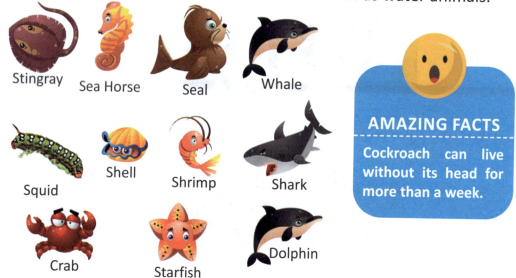

Stingray   Sea Horse   Seal   Whale

Squid   Shell   Shrimp   Shark

Crab   Starfish   Dolphin

AMAZING FACTS

Cockroach can live without its head for more than a week.

8. **Land Animals:** Animals that live on land are known as land animals.

Lion   Tiger   Elephant

Cow   Cat   Dog

9. **Farm Animals:** Animals that are reared in farms to obtain useful things from them are known as farm animals.

Plants and Animals

★ **Animals and Their Homes**

★ **Animals and Their Young Ones**

Bear-Cub	Butterfly-Caterpilar	Cat-Kitten
Cow-Calf	Deer-Fawn	Dog-Puppy
Duck-Duckling	Elephant-Calf	Frog-Tadpole
Hen-Chick	Horse-Foal	Pig-Piglet
Rabbit-Bunny	Sheep-Lamb	Tiger-Cub

★ **Animals and their Sounds**

Animals	Sounds
Dog	Bark
Cat	Meow
Cow	Moo
Lion	Roar
Tiger	Roar
Goat	Bleat
Elephant	Trumpet
Horse	Neigh

Plants and Animals

Monkey	Chatter
Bird	Chirp
Duck	Quack
Bee	Buzz/Hum
Owl	Hoot
Snake	Hiss

★ **Animals and Their Group names**

Animals	Group Names
Lion	Pride
Bee	Swarm
Ant	Colony
Bird	Flock
Cattle	Herd
Fish	School
Elephant	Herd

★ **Taking Care of Animals**

1. Do not throw stones at animals.
2. Do not keep birds in cages.
3. Take proper care of them and love them.
4. Give them enough food, fresh water, etc.

Multiple Choice Questions

LEVEL 1

1. Which of these animals lives on tree?

    (a) Eagle
    (b)  Flying fish
    (c) Octopus
    (d) Penguin

    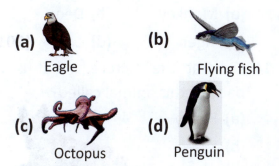

    [2019]

2. Select the incorrect match.

	Animal		Sound
(a)	Cow	–	Moo
(b)	Horse	–	Neigh
(c)	Crow	–	Coo
(d)	Elephant	–	Trumpet

    [2019]

47

3. Select the correct match.

	Animal		Young One
(a)	Butterfly	–	Silkworm
(b)	Kangaroo	–	Kid
(c)	Elephant	–	Cub
(d)	Frog	–	Tadpole

[2019]

4. Which of the following is the most colourful part of a plant which changes into fruit?
   (a) Root (b) Leaves
   (c) Flower (d) Stem [2017]

5. Which of the following is the fastest running animal?
   (a) Lion (b) Cheetah
   (c) Dog (d) Rabbit [2017]

6. Which of the following is a creeper?

   (a)
   Pumpkin

   (b)
   Money plant

   (c)
   Grapevine

   (d)
   Bean [2016]

7. Which of the following is the green part of a plant where food is made?
   (a) Root (b) Shoot
   (c) Leaves (d) Stem [2016]

8.
   These animals are _____.
   (a) Farm animals
   (b) Wild animals
   (c) Water animals
   (d) Domestic animals [2016]

9. From the given box, count and answer the total number of domestic animals, birds and water animals.

Cow	Hen	Lion	Parrot
Ostrich	Rabbit	Butterfly	Dolphin

   (a) 3 (b) 4
   (c) 6 (d) 2 [2016]

10. Which of the following plant have strong and woody branches?
    (a) Mango
    (b) Money plant
    (c) Neem
    (d) Both (a) and (c) [2015]

11. Which of the following parts of a plant provides support to the upper part of a pant?
    (a) Root (b) Shoot
    (c) Stem (d) Leaf [2015]

12. Which of the following is a WRONG match of animal and its home?
    (a) Cat-Kennel
    (b) Horse-Stable
    (c) Rabbit- Hutch
    (d) Tiger-Lair [2015]

13. Which of the following will you find in forests, jumping on the trees?
    (a) Monkey (b) Deer
    (c) Tiger (d) Cow [2015]

14. Look at the picture. What is the baby of this animal called?
    (a) Puppy
    (b) Kitten
    (c) Cub
    (d) Calf

15. Which animal gives us milk?
    (a) Hen   (b) Cow
    (c) Dog   (d) Bee
16. Which of these is a domestic animal?

    (a)

    (b)

    (c)

    (d)

17. Name the fruit shown in the given picture.
    (a) Pineapple
    (b) Mango
    (c) Banana
    (d) Pomegranate
18. Name the tree shown in the given picture.
    (a) Banyan
    (b) Coconut
    (c) Neem
    (d) Peepal

19. Which of these animals lives in water as well as on land?
    (a) Dolphin   (b) Crocodile
    (c) Lion   (d) Jelly fish
20. This animal is the main source of wool from which we make warm clothes for the winter. Name the animal.
    (a) Goat   (b) Sheep
    (c) Cow   (d) Cat
21. Choose the odd one out.
    (a) Lion   (b) Fox
    (c) Sheep   (d) Dolphin
22. Which of the following is not an aquatic animal?
    (a) Starfish   (b) Whale
    (c) Dolphin   (d) Deer
23. Which of the following is NOT a herb?

    (a)
    Coriander

    (b)
    Wheat

    (c)
    Grass

    (d)
    Tulsi

24. This part of a plant bears leaf, flower, and fruit. Identify the part. Identify it.
(a) Root
(b) Stem
(c) Shoot
(d) None of the above

25. Which of the following is an example of climbers?
(a) Cucumber
(b) Bottle gourd
(c) Pumpkin
(d) Grapevine

LEVEL 2

1. Give a group name for the following set of words.

| Mosquito, Bee, Fly, Butterfly, Wasp |

(a) Sea creatures
(b) Insects
(c) Dogs
(d) Tools [2019]

2. Select the correct match

(a)

(b)

(c)

(d)

[2018]

3.
| A dog likes to bark |
| Mostly at the park |
| A cow likes to ____ |
| But it does not have a clue |

Which of the following words will complete the given rhyme?
(a) Blue
(b) Coo
(c) Moo
(d) Boo [2018]

4. What is a group of puppies called?
(a) Litter   (b) Swarm
(c) School   (d) Pride [2018]

5. Monkey can jump and climb trees
Giraffes are tall and they eat leaves
Parrot are colourful and they can _____ .
Elephants can't but would love to try.
Which of the following words will complete the given rhyme?
(a) Dye   (b) Fly
(c) Ply   (d) Buy [2018]

6. "You do not have this but a dog has one which it wags to show that it is happy."
The answer to the above riddle is _____.
(a) Hand   (b) Tail
(c) Tongue (d) Paw
[2018]

Plants and Animals

7. A group of crocodiles is called a/an _____.
   (a) Army
   (b) Float
   (c) Pod
   (d) Tower [2018]

8. An apple is a _____. It contains _____ inside it which give rise to a new _____.
   (a) Seed, fruit, flower
   (b) Fruit, seeds, leaves
   (c) Fruit, leaves, fruit
   (d) Fruit, seeds, plant [2017]

9. Match the phrases with the given words.

	List-1		List-2
A.	Peacock	1.	Water animal
B.	Octopus	2.	Bird
C.	Insect	3.	Land animal
D.	Sheep	4.	Fly

	A	B	C	D
(a)	2	1	4	3
(b)	4	2	3	1
(c)	3	2	1	4
(d)	4	3	1	2

[2017]

10. Which one of the following is called the King of Fruits?

    (a) Mango
    (b) Apple
    (c) Papaya
    (d) Banana

11. Which of the following statements is true?
    (a) Pineapple is a vegetable.
    (b) Pumpkin is a vegetable.
    (c) Wheat is a vegetable.
    (d) Guava is a vegetable. [2016]

12. Which of the following options will replace 'X' and 'Y' in the table.

Fruits	Apple	Papaya
Herbs	Coriander	'X'
Grains	'Y'	Maize

    (a) X-Potato, Y-Rice
    (b) X-Tulsi, Y-Papaya
    (c) X-Spinach, Y-Rice
    (d) X- Pumpkin, Y-Rice [2016]

13. Amit has two animals. They both are very useful to Amit. One gives milk and other is used for travelling from one place to another. Which of the following animals does Amit have?
    (a) Cow and Lion
    (b) Goat and hen
    (d) Cow and horse
    (d) Cow and deer [2016]

14. Arrange the following sentences in correct order.
    1. Cut the fruits safely with knife.
    2. Clean your hands first.
    3. Wash the fruits.
    4. Eat fruits as they keep us healthy.
    (a) 1-2-3-4
    (b) 2-3-4-1
    (c) 4-3-2-1

(d) 2-3-1-4 **[2015]**

15. Which of the following activities we should avoid?
    (a) Grow more and more plants in the garden.
    (b) Give proper water to plants.
    (c) Pluck flower and leaves from the plant.
    (d) Throw garbage and waste in the dustbin. **[2015]**

16. Which of the following parts of a plant gives rise to a new plant?
    (a) Leaf
    (b) Root
    (c) Seed
    (d) Flower **[2015]**

17. Identify 'Y':

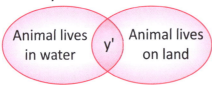

    (a) Monkey   (b) Dolphin
    (c) Frog   (d) Lion **[2015]**

18. Read the following statements and choose the correct answer.
    1. Dog is a pet animal.
    2. Dog is a land animal.
    3. Dog protects our home.
    4. Dog lives in a lair.
    (a) Statement 1 & 4 are false, statements 2 & 3 are true.
    (b) Statements 1, 2 & 3 are true, statement 4 is false.
    (c) Statements 1 & 2 are true, statements 3 & 4 are false.
    (d) All the statements are true.

19. Which of the following is NOT true about animals?
    (a) Pet animals live with us.
    (b) Arial animals can fly.
    (c) All animals live on land.
    (d) Wild animals live in jungle.

20. How many names of animals are hidden in the given word grid?

M	O	N	K	E	Y	C	R
W	P	S	J	L	A	F	B
C	O	W	N	E	K	N	E
D	I	U	K	P	G	T	A
F	O	X	O	H	B	D	R
Q	H	C	Z	A	E	E	P
L	I	O	N	N	V	E	L
A	M	Y	U	T	I	R	X

    (a) 4   (b) 6
    (c) 8   (d) 10

ACHIEVERS SECTION

1. Study the table.

Trees	Shrubs	Climbers/Creepers
Banyan	Rose	Cucumber
Mango	1	2

   1 and 2 can respectively be
   (a) Orange and Marigold
   (b) Neem and tulsi
   (c) Hibiscus and pumpkin
   (d) Lotus and apple **[2019]**

Plants and Animals

2. In a famous fairy tale, the Fairy Godmother turned _____ into a coach so that Cinderella could go to the Prince's Ball.
   (a) Mouse (b) Potato
   (c) Pumpkin (d) Cockroach
   [2018]

3. The name of which of the following leaves is NOT found in the word gird?

Y	T	U	L	I	P	K	J	T	B
S	U	N	F	L	O	W	E	R	A
F	M	A	N	G	O	M	E	Q	N
I	L	Q	E	T	H	C	O	B	Y
R	D	N	E	X	L	S	S	Z	A
K	I	R	M	U	V	L	E	P	N
C	O	C	O	N	U	T	F	G	F
T	U	P	E	E	P	A	L	B	C

   (a)   (b)
   (c)   (d)
   [2018]

4. The name of which of the following flowers is NOT found in the gird?

R	Q	O	L	I	M	N	L	K	W
A	C	H	I	N	A	R	O	S	E
T	S	R	L	P	R	H	T	I	T
W	R	A	Y	E	I	L	U	L	O
V	I	N	A	O	G	L	S	E	T
O	A	I	S	Y	O	G	E	W	F
P	U	R	P	L	L	E	H	L	O
N	X	G	K	A	D	G	O	R	O

   (a)   (b)
   (c)   (d)
   [2018]

5. Unscramble the jumbled letters to find a word which means 'A group of fish'.

   HOSLA

   (a) Alohs (b) Loash
   (c) Shoal (d) Sloah **[2018]**

Answer-Key

LEVEL 1

1. (a)	2. (c)	3. (d)	4. (c)	5. (b)
6. (a)	7. (c)	8. (b)	9. (c)	10. (d)
11. (c)	12. (a)	13. (a)	14. (a)	15. (b)
16. (d)	17. (a)	18. (a)	19. (b)	20. (b)
21. (d)	22. (d)	23. (d)	24. (b)	25. (d)

General Knowledge One For All Olympiads Solved Papers, Class-1

LEVEL 2

1. (b)	2. (b)	3. (c)	4. (a)	5. (b)
6. (b)	7. (b)	8. (d)	9. (a)	10. (a)
11. (b)	12. (c)	13. (c)	14. (d)	15. (c)
16. (c)	17. (c)	18. (b)	19. (c)	20. (c)

ACHIEVERS SECTION

| 1. (c) | 2. (c) | 3. (c) | 4. (b) | 5. (c) |

Answers with Explanation

LEVEL 1

1. **Correct option is (a)**
   Explanation: Eagle is a bird that flies in air and lives on a tree.

2. **Correct option is (c)**
   Explanation: The sound of Crow is Caw.

3. **Correct option is (d)**
   Explanation:
   Butterfly – Caterpillar
   Kangaroo – Joey
   Elephant – Calf
   Frog – Tadpole

4. **Correct option is (c)**
   Explanation: Flower is the most colourful part of a plant. It changes into fruits as it is also the reproductive part of the plant.

5. **Correct option is (b)**
   Explanation: Cheetah is the fastest running animal and its speed is around 120 km per hour.

6. **Correct option is (a)**
   Explanation: Pumpkin plant is a creeper as it spreads on the ground.

7. **Correct option is (c)**
   Explanation: Leaves are the green part of a plant which make food for the plant.

8. **Correct option is (b)**
   Explanation: Bear, lion and tiger are wild animals.

9. **Correct option is (c)**
   Explanation: Total number of domestic animals, birds and water animals is – 6.
   Domestic animals – Cow, Rabbit (2)
   Birds – Hen, Parrot, Ostrich (3)
   Water animals – Dolphin (1)

54

Plants and Animals

10. Correct option is (d)
Explanation: Mango and Neem plant have strong and woody branches, whereas, money plant has a soft stem.

11. Correct option is (c)
Explanation: Stem provides support to the upper part of a plant. It bears leaves, flowers and fruits.

12. Correct option is (a)
Explanation: Cat lives in cattery or cat house.

13. Correct option is (a)
Explanation: Monkeys are wild animals. They live on trees. They can be found in cities, villages, and jungle.

14. Correct option is (a)
Explanation: Puppy is the young one of dog.

15. Correct option is (b)
Explanation: Cow gives us milk. Bee gives us honey. Hen gives us meat and egg. Dog guards our house.

16. Correct option is (d
Explanation: Cow is a domestic animal as it can be tamed to obtain useful things. Lion, bear, and deer are wild animals as they live in the forest.

19. Correct option is (b)
Explanation: Dolphin lives in water. Crocodile lives in water as well as on land. Lion is a land animal. Jelly fish is a water animal.

20. Correct option is (b)
Explanation: Sheep gives us wool from which woollen clothes are made.

21. Correct option is (d)
Explanation: Lion, fox and sheep live on land, whereas, dolphin lives in water.

22. Correct option is (d)
Explanation: Deer is a land animal, whereas starfish, whole and dolphin are water animals.

23. Correct option is (d)
Explanation: Tulsi is a shrub, whereas coriander wheat and grass a herbal.

25. Correct option is (d)
Explanation: Cucumber, bottle gourd and pumpkin spread along the ground, thus they all are creepers. Grapevine grows vertically up with then on some support, thus it is a climber.

LEVEL 2

1. **Correct option is (b)**
   Explanation: Mosquito, bee, fly, butterfly, wasp, etc., are all insects as they are small in size, have 6 legs and one or two pair of wings.

2. **Correct option is (b)**
   Explanation: Sheep gives us wool from which we make warm clothes for winter.

3. **Correct option is (c)**
   Explanation:

Animal	Sound
Cow	Moo

4. **Correct option is (a)**
   Explanation:

Animal	Group names
Puppies	Litter
Bees	Swarm
Fish	School/Shoal
Lions	Pride

5. **Correct option is (b)**
   Explanation: Parrot is a bird that flies in the air.

6. **Correct option is (b)**
   Explanation: Dogs have tail that they wag when they are happy. Humans do not have a tail.

8. **Correct option is (d)**
   Explanation: An apple is a fruit. It contains seeds inside it which give rise to a new plant.

9. **Correct option is (a)**
   Explanation: Peacock is a bird. Octopus is a water animal.
   Fly is on insects.
   Sheep is a land animal.

10. **Correct option is (a)**
    Explanation: Mango is called the 'King of Fruits' as it is nutritionally rich and has a unique flavor.

11. **Correct option is (b)**
    Explanation: Pineapple and guava are fruits. Pumpkin is a vegetable. Wheat is a grain.

13. **Correct option is (c)**
    Explanation: Cow gives us milk and horse is used for travelling from one place to another.

14. **Correct option is (d)**
    Explanation: We should first clean our hands. Then wash the fruit. After washing the fruit, we should cut the fruit safely with a knife. At last, eat the fruit as it keeps us healthy.

15. **Correct option is (c)**
    Explanation: We should not pluck flowers and leaves from the plant as flowers get converted into fruits and leaves prepare food for the plant.

17. **Correct option is (c)**
    Explanation: Frog lives on land as well as in water.

18. **Correct option is (b)**
    Explanation: Dog lives in a kennel.

Plants and Animals

19. Correct option is (c)
    Explanation: Some animals live on land, some live in water and some live on both land and in water.

20. Correct option is (c)
    Explanation: Monkey, Cow, Ox, Elephant, Yak, Deer, Bear, Lion

ACHIEVERS SECTION

1. Correct option is (c)
   Explanation: Shrubs are small and bushy plants, for example, hibiscus, rose, tulsi, etc.
   Creepers grow along the ground, for example, pumpkin, watermelon, muskmelon, etc.

3. Correct option is (c)
   Explanation: Option 'c' is a leaf of banana tree.

4. Correct option is (b)
   Explanation: Option 'b' is sunflower.

5. Correct option is (c)
   Explanation: Name for a group of fishes is shoal.

How to make learning
Fun, Effective & Responsive
at the same time?

It's easy!
Scan the QR codes below

Animals Around Us   Parts of Plants   Types of Plants
and get started!

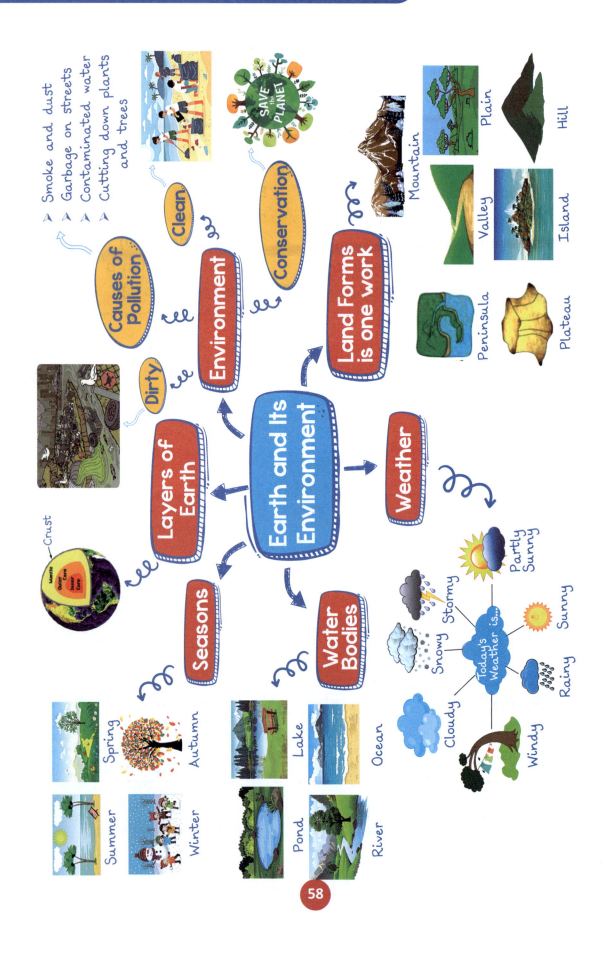

CHAPTER 3
EARTH AND ITS ENVIRONMENT

Learning Outcomes

Children would be able to:
- ✓ Explain the uniqueness of the Earth in the Solar System;
- ✓ Reflect positively on the necessity of a clean environment;
- ✓ Inculcate healthy habits related to environment;

Concept Review

INTRODUCTION

We all are a part of this Earth and its our responsibility to keep the environment clean and protect our planet. This chapter makes children understand that the Earth is a celestial body and an important part of the Solar System. It makes them appreciate their immediate surroundings and the importance of hygiene and cleanliness.

Earth

- Our Earth is our mother as it fulfills all of our needs such as food, water and other things.
- It is round in shape, but a slight flattened on the top and bottom like an orange. It is not flat as we see it.
- We live on its surface which is made up of water and land.
- It is covered by a layer of air.
- We live on the land, which is not same everywhere.

AMAZING FACTS

Earth is the third planet from the Sun in our Solar System. Its name comes from the old English and Germanic words meaning 'the ground'.

- Most of the part of the Earth is covered with water, which includes oceans, seas, rivers, lakes, etc.
- Our planet, Earth, is unique as it has the best combination of land, water and air required to sustain life.

★ **Layers of Earth**
1. **Crust:** Solid outer layer of Earth on which we live.
2. **Mantle:** Under the crust lies the mantle. This layer is made up of molten rock.
3. **Core:** Deepest and hottest layer of Earth.

★ **What Earth Looks Like**
- Only our planet sustains life. It has about 70% water and 30% land.
- It is a beautiful planet and looks blue when viewed from space because it has lots of water.
- Earth has seven major landmasses which are known as **continents**. (The continents from largest to smallest are: Asia, Africa, North America, South America, Antarctica, Europe, and Australia.)
- We find mountains, valleys and plains on the Earth's surface as different landforms.
- A large elevated part of the Earth is called a **mountain**.

- **Hill** is also a raised area on the surface of the Earth but it is not as high and steep as a mountain.

AMAZING FACTS

Nearly 97% of the world's water is salty or undrinkable.

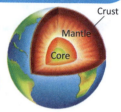

AMAZING FACTS
- Mountain animals have sharp hooves that help them to climb mountains.
- Mount Everest is the highest mountain in the world.

Earth and Its Environment

- A **valley** is a long depression or low land between mountains and hills.

DID YOU KNOW?

Some plains are formed by the action of rivers, these are called river plains.

- A large flat area on the surface of Earth is called **plains**.

FUN TRIVIA

Earth is 4.543 billion years old even it is strong enough to hold all of us.

- A land mass surrounded by water on its three sides and connected to land on one side is called **peninsula**.

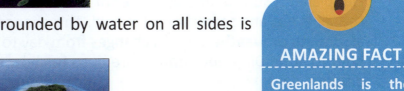

AMAZING FACT

Greenlands is the largest island in the world.

- A land mass surrounded by water on all sides is called an **island**.

DID YOU KNOW?

Plateaus are usually good for growing certain crops.

- A **plateau** is a high land on the Earth surface, which is almost flat at the top.

61

★ **Water Bodies**
- All living things need water in order to survive. Water on Earth is available as fresh water and salty water. Water lakes, ponds, rivers, etc., are known as fresh-water bodies. While oceans and seas are known as salt water bodies. Oceans, are the largest water bodies. Many plants and animals live in the ocean as well. There are five oceans, separated by different continents, namely the Pacific, Atlantic, Indian, Southern (Antarctic), and Arctic Oceans (in descending order by area).

River   Pond   Lake

Ocean

AMAZING FACTS

The Nile river in Africa is the longest river in the world.

★ **Weather and Seasons**
- Our planet is surrounded by a layer of air called the atmosphere. Sometimes this air is hot and sometimes it is cold. This change in atmosphere is known as **climate** or **weather**, which changes from day to day and sometimes from hour to hour. Different symbols are used to show the weather condition on different days:

Rainy   Snowy   Sunny

Cloudy   Thunderstorm   Partly Sunny

- When the weather remains unchanged for a long period of time, we call it a **season.** We have some months when it rains very heavily, some months when it is very hot, some months when it is very cold and some months when it is neither too hot nor too cold.

★ **There are four main seasons:**

1. **Summer**
   - The sun shines very brightly, hence this is the hottest season
   - April, May and June are the months of summer season.
   - People like to have cold water, cold drinks, juices and ice-cream, etc.
   - People prefer to wear cotton clothes.

2. **Monsoon**
   - It comes after summer.
   - July and August are the months of monsoon season.
   - Rain and clouds come with cold winds and sometimes with thunder storms.
   - Trees and plants look greener during this season.
   - People use umbrella, raincoats, etc., to keep themselves from getting wet.
   - Sometimes use also sea a rainbow immediately often a rain.

DID YOU KNOW?

June 21 marks the day when the Earth is turned the most towards the Sun. This is known as Summer Solstice. It is the longest, sunniest day of the year.

3. **Autumn**
   - It comes after monsoon season.
   - September and October are the months of autumn season.
   - It is neither hot nor too cold.
   - Leaves of most of the plants turn yellow, get dry and then fall down.

4. **Winter**
   - It is cold and chilly.
   - November, December and January are months of winter season.
   - People mostly wear warm or woollen clothes.

DID YOU KNOW?

December 21 marks the day when the Earth is turned the farthest from the Sun. This is known as Winter Solstice. It is the shortest, day of the year.

5. **Spring**
   - It is neither too hot nor too cold.
   - The days are very pleasant.
   - February and March are the months of spring season.
   - Trees and plants have fresh leaves and colourful flowers.

DID YOU KNOW?

Trees and plants open new leaves and flower buds as the weather warms up in spring.

 Environment

- Everything around us is known as Environment. It includes both living things like humans, plants, animals, etc. and non-living things like water, air, food, etc.

Clean Environment

Dirty Environment

★ Causes of Environmental Pollution
- Mixing of smoke and dust in the air.
- Throwing garbage on street.
- Contamination water due to throwing wastes into it.
- Cutting down of plants and trees.

★ Conservation of Environment: Reduce, Reuse and Recycle (3Rs)
1. **Reduce:** By reducing the consumption of materials that pollute the environment, we can reduce the waste we create.
2. **Reuse:** By using the items again and again for the same purpose.
3. **Recycle:** By converting old products into new ones.

Multiple Choice Questions

LEVEL 1

1. A piece of land surrounded by water on three sides is called a _____ and a piece of land surrounded by water on all sides is called a/an _____.
   (a) Peninsula, island
   (b) Lake, island
   (c) Pond, lake
   (d) River, lake   **[2019]**

2. Which of the following on unscrambling will give the name of the largest island in the world?
   (a) ENERLNADG
   (b) UABC
   (c) ADLNIEC
   (d) NAJPA   **[2019]**

3. Which of the following is the largest continent in the world?
   (a) Australia   (b) Asia
   (c) Antarctica   (d) Africa

4. Which season is shown in the given picture?

   (a) Summer   (b) Autumn
   (c) Spring   (d) Winter

5. In which of the following seasons, we prefer to wear cotton clothes?
   (a) Summer   (b) Autumn
   (c) Spring   (d) Winter

6. The seven large landmasses on the Earth are called_____.
   (a) Island
   (b) Mountain
   (c) Continents
   (d) Peninsula

7. Match the Column I with Column II.

Column I		Column II	
A.	🌸	1.	Summer
B.	🌳	2.	Winter
C.	🍂	3.	Autumn
D.	🌲	4.	Spring

(a) A-4, B-1, C-3, D-2
(b) A-1, B-2, C-3, D-4
(c) A-4, B-3, C-2, D-1
(d) A-2, B-1, C-3, D-4

8. Which of the following will help to keep our environment clean?
   (a) Do not throw garbage on the street.
   (b) Do not waste paper.
   (c) Plant more and more trees.
   (d) All of the above.

9. In which of the following seasons, weather is neither too hot nor too cold?
   (a) Spring
   (b) Summer
   (c) Winter
   (d) None of the above

10. What should we do to save our Earth?
    (a) We should not turn on the lights all day.
    (b) We should not kill or hurt animals in the wild.
    (c) We should not use recycled paper.
    (d) Both (a) and (b)

11. _____ is the uppermost layer of the Earth.
    (a) Crust
    (b) Mantle
    (c) Core
    (d) None of the above

12. To cut down on the use of resources is _____.
    (a) Reduce
    (b) Reuse
    (c) Recycle
    (d) None of the above

13. Moving a called _____.
    (a) Wind
    (b) Light
    (c) Sunshine
    (d) None of the above

14. Identify the land form shown in the given picture.

Earth and Its Environment

(a) Plateau (b) Mountain
(c) Plain   (d) Valley

15. _____ covers most of our Earth.
    (a) Land
    (b) Water
    (c) Sand
    (d) Salt

16. How many oceans are on Earth?
    (a) 7   (b) 5
    (c) 3   (d) 6

17. Which of the following is a water body?
    (a) Peninsula
    (b) Plateau
    (c) Mountain
    (d) Lake

18. Identify the water body shown in the given picture.

    (a) Pond   (b) River
    (c) Lake   (d) Ocean

19. How much percentage of Earth is covered with water?
    (a) 70%   (b) 30%
    (c) 50%   (d) 10%

20. Which of the following is often seen often a rainfall?
    (a) Night
    (b) Rainbow
    (c) Snowfall
    (d) Both (a) and (c)

LEVEL 2

1. Most of Earth's freshwater is in:
   (a) Oceans
   (b) Atmosphere
   (c) Rivers, lakes, streams, etc.
   (d) All of the above

2. Which of the following is an INCORRECT match?

(a)	Plains	Flat areas of land
(b)	Hill	Raised area of land
(c)	Valley	Dry area of land
(d)	Mountain	Highest landform

3. Match the following.

	Column I		Column II
A.	☁️	1.	Rainy
B.	🌧️	2.	Cloudy
C.	⛈️	3.	Sunny
D.	☀️	4.	Thunder Storm

(a) A-1, B-2, C-4, D-3
(b) A-2, B-1, C-3, D-4
(c) A-2, B-1, C-4, D-3
(d) A-4, B-1, C-2, D-3

4. Match the following and select the correct option.

Column I		Column II
A. (plastic bag)		1. GLASS
B. (newspaper)		2. PLASTIC
C. (glass bottle)		3. METAL
D. (metal can)		4. PAPER

(a) A-2, B-4, C-1, D-3
(b) A-4, B-3, C-1, D-2
(c) A-3, B-2, C-1, D-4
(d) A-2, B-1, C-4, D-3

5. Weather always:
(a) Changes
(b) Never changes
(c) Stays for a long time
(d) All of the above

6. Which part of the Earth is the hottest?
(a) Core
(b) Crust
(c) Mantle
(d) None of the above

7. Paper can be _____ and that paper can be used to make newspaper.
(a) Made (b) Planted
(c) Destroyed (d) Recycled

8. It is a sunny day. Rahul feels hot standing outside in the sun. He has an umbrella. Rahul opens the umbrella and stands under it.

Identify the season.
(a) Summer (b) Winter
(c) Monsoon (d) Autumn

9. Which is the smallest continent in the world?
(a) Australia (b) Africa
(c) Asia (d) Europe

10. Which is the longest river in the world?
(a) Ganges (b) Amazon river
(c) Nile (d) Danube river

11. Name the highest mountain in the world.
    (a) Mount K2
    (b) Mount Kanchenjunga
    (c) Mount Manaslu
    (d) Mount Everest

12. _____ is the largest ocean in the world.
    (a) Indian Ocean
    (b) Atlantic Ocean
    (c) Pacific Ocean
    (d) Arctic Ocean

13. 3Rs rule for conservation of environment means:
    (a) Resize, redesign and reject
    (b) Reduce, reuse and recycle
    (c) Reject, reuse and refuse
    (d) Reduce, refill and restart

14. People keep _____ out of the river to keep the water clean.
    (a) Wastes   (b) Sand
    (c) Fishes   (d) Plants

15. Which of the following options will replace 'X' and 'Y' in the given table.

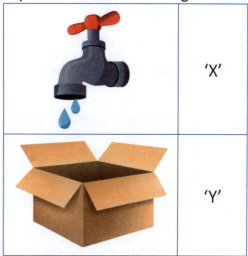

    (a) X-Reduce, Y-Reuse
    (b) X-Reuse, Y-Reduce
    (c) X-Recycle, Y-Reduce
    (d) None of the above

ACHIEVERS SECTION

1. How many names of landforms are hidden in the given word grid?

M	A	U	N	T	A	I	N	S	X
A	B	X	Z	V	A	L	L	E	Y
D	R	S	A	M	K	B	C	V	P
X	B	H	I	L	L	S	Q	N	L
Z	O	N	T	P	R	D	H	T	A
P	L	A	T	E	A	U	J	L	I
A	V	K	W	X	F	I	Q	S	N

    (a) Three   (b) Five
    (c) Seven   (d) Nine

2. Radha went to be market with her mother. She bought a bottle of packed drinking water as she was felling thirsty. Now she used that bottle for watering plants. Which of the following method did she use to help our ecosystem?
    (a) Reduce
    (b) Reuse
    (c) Recycle
    (d) None of the above

3. Read the following statements and choose the correct answer.
   1. Hill is a raised area of land but not as high and steep as a mountain.
   2. We live on the solid outer layer of the Earth.
   3. Freshwater is salty.
   4. All planets support life.
   (a) Statements 1 and 2 are true, statements 3 and 4 are false.
   (b) Statements 1 and 2 are false, statements 3 and 4 are true.
   (c) Statements 1, 2 and 3 are true, statement 4 is false.
   (d) Statements 1, 2 and 4 are true, statement 3 is false.
4. I turn off the water when I brush my teeth. Which of the following conservation method of natural resources has been used?
   (a) Reduce
   (b) Reuse
   (c) Recycle
   (d) None of the above
5. Read the following statements and find true/false.
   1. Pond is a very small water body surrounded by land.
   2. Ocean is a huge water body that covers large part of the Earth.
   3. River is a large water body containing salty water.
   4. Lakes are not surrounded by land.
   (a) T,T,F,T
   (b) T,F,T,F
   (c) T,T,F,F
   (d) F,T,F,F

Answer-Key

LEVEL 1

1. (a)	2. (a)	3. (b)	4. (b)	5. (a)
6. (c)	7. (a)	8. (d)	9. (a)	10. (d)
11. (a)	12. (a)	13. (a)	14. (b)	15. (b)
16. (b)	17. (d)	18. (a)	19. (a)	20. (b)

LEVEL 2

1. (c)	2. (c)	3. (c)	4. (a)	5. (a)
6. (a)	7. (d)	8. (a)	9. (a)	10. (c)
11. (d)	12. (c)	13. (b)	14. (a)	15. (a)

Earth and Its Environment

ACHIEVERS SECTION

| 1. (b) | 2. (b) | 3. (a) | 4. (a) | 5. (c) |

Answers with Explanations

LEVEL 1

1. **Correct option is (a)**
   Explanation: A piece of land surrounded by water on three sides is called a peninsula, whereas island is surrounded by water on all sides.

2. **Correct option is (a)**
   Explanation: Largest Island: Greenland

4. **Correct option is (b)**
   Explanation: In autumn season, leaves first turn yellow and then fall off from trees.

5. **Correct option is (a)**
   Explanation: We prefer to wear cotton clothes in the summer season to keep ourselves cool.

6. **Correct option is (c)**
   Explanation: Continents are large landmasses found on Earth. They are seven in number.

9. **Correct option is (a)**
   Explanation: Weather is too hot in summer and too cold in winter. Weather is neither too hot nor too cold in spring.

10. **Correct option is (d)**
    Explanation: We should use recycled paper to save our Earth.

11. **Correct option is (a)**
    Explanation: Crust is the uppermost layer of Earth on which we live.

12. **Correct option is (a)**
    Explanation: Reduce is to cut down the use of resources in order to reduce the generation of waste.

13. **Correct option is (a)**
    Explanation: Moving air is called Wind.

14. **Correct option is (b)**
    Explanation: Mountain is an elevated part of land which is very high and steep.

15. **Correct option is (b)**
    Explanation: Water covers approximately. 70 % part of our Earth.

16. **Correct option is (b)**
    Explanation: Earth has five oceans namely Pacific ocean, Atlantic ocean, Indian ocean, Southern ocean, and Arctic ocean.

17. **Correct option is (d)**
    Explanation: Peninsula, plateau, and mountain are landforms.
18. **Correct option is (a)**
    Explanation: Pond is a very small water body having freshwater.
19. **Correct option is (a)**
    Explanation: 70% of Earth is covered with water, while 30% is covered with land.
20. **Correct option is (b)**
    Explanation: A rainbow is often seen after a rainfall.

LEVEL 2

1. **Correct option is (c)**
   Explanation: Rivers, lakes and streams are the source of fresh water, whereas, ocean has salty water. Atmosphere is the air around us.
2. **Correct option is (c)**
   Explanation: Valley is the low land area between mountains or hills.
5. **Correct option is (a)**
   Explanation: Weather always changes, whereas season stays for a long time.
6. **Correct option is (a)**
   Explanation: Core is the hottest layer of the Earth having temperature of approximately. 50,000 degree Celsius.
7. **Correct option is (d)**
   Explanation: Paper can be recycled and that paper can be used to make other products such as newspaper, boxes, etc.
8. **Correct option is (a)**
   Explanation: It is a sunny day means Sun is bright and hot. Rahul opens his umbrella to protect himself from the Sun. Thus, it is summer season.
13. **Correct option is (b)**
    Explanation: 3Rs:
    Reduce: Cutting down the use of resources
    Reuse: Using the resources again for the same purpose
    Recycle: Converting old products into new ones
14. **Correct option is (a)**
    Explanation: We keep wastes out of the river to keep the water clean.
15. **Correct option is (a)**
    Explanation: We can reduce the usage of water by turning off the tap.
    We can reuse the carton to carry things from one place to another or to store things.

ACHIEVERS SECTION

1. **Correct option is (b)**
   Explanation: Mountain, Hill, Valley, Plateau, Plain.

2. **Correct option is (b)**
   Explanation: Reusing water bottle again for different purposes helps to save the environment.

3. **Correct option is (a)**
   Explanation: Freshwater does not taste salty.
   Only our planet Earth supports life.

4. **Correct option is (a)**
   Explanation: Turning off the water when we brush our teeth helps to reduce the amount of water we use.

5. **Correct option is (c)**
   Explanation: Rivers are large water bodies of fresh water.
   Lakes are surrounded by land.

How to make learning
Fun, Effective & Responsive
at the same time?

It's easy!
Scan the QR codes below

Our Earth   Layers of Earth   Weather and Seasons

and get started!

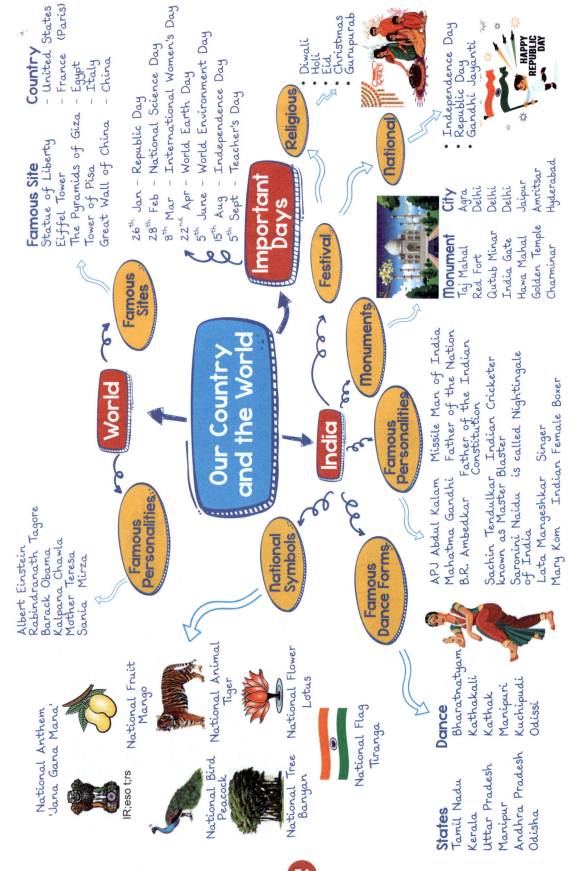

CHAPTER 4
OUR COUNTRY AND THE WORLD

Learning Outcomes

Children would be able to:
- Recognize national symbols of India;
- Recognize and name various types of Indian clothing, dances, festivals;
- Recognize various monuments and famous places in India and the World;
- Identify various famous personalities in India and the World;
- Recognize and distinguish between flags of different countries;
- Know some important days.

Concept Review

INTRODUCTION

Being a part of this world, we must know at least the most important facts about our world. India is our country which is known for its unity in diversity. Diversity in region, food, religion, festival, languages, etc., are seen in India. This chapter familiarizes and inculcates a sense of respect among children for the country's and world's rich national, historical and cultural heritage.

Our Country

India is a part of Asia. It is the seventh largest country in the world. India has the second highest population in the world. The capital of India is New Delhi.

DID YOU KNOW?

India has no official religion, but more than 80% of Indians are Hindu. About 13% are Muslim. Other religions include Christianity, Buddhism, Sikhism and Jainism, are also practiced in India.

Festivals

A festival is an occasion of celebration or feasting. We celebrate various festivals in our country. Some of them are:

★ Religious Festivals

FUN TRIVIA

India is the second most populated and it is managed by the longest constitution in the world. Also it is at top to celebrate with maximum number of festivals.

1. **Diwali:** Diwali is a festival of lights. On this day People decorate their houses with clay lamps and candles. People also wear new clothes and worship Goddess Lakshmi. Family members give sweets and gifts to each other.

2. **Holi:** Holi is a festival of colours as we play holi by applying 'Gulal' and throwing coloured water on each other. People prepare *gujiya*, *mathri*, *thandai*, etc. for family members, close friends and relatives.

3. **Eid:** Eid is celebrated by people who follow the Islam religion. It is celebrated after the completion of 30 days long fast of Ramadan. People wear new clothes, exchange gifts with each other and greet each other with 'Eid Mubark' and formal embraces. They also distribute food to needy people. People also pray in large groups in the mosque and prepare delicious '*meethi sevaiyaan*'.

4. **Christmas:** Christmas is celebrated by Christians on 25th December every year to honour the birthday of Jesus Christ. People wear new clothes, decorate Christmas tree, exchange gifts and eat festive meals.

5. **Gurpurab:** Gurpurab is celebrated to honour the birthday of Guru Nanak Dev. This day is also know as Guru Nanak Jayanti. It is celebrated by Sikhs. People wear new clothes, pray in Gurudwara and arrange free langers for all.

6. **Lohri:** It is celebrated mostly by the Punjabis and by the people living in the Northern part of India. The festival celebrates the cropping season as well as bidding goodbye to the chilling winters. People do bonfire and sing and dance around it. People also eat sweets made of til, jaggery, etc., on this day.

7. **Raksha Bhandhan:** It is a festival of celebrating love and duty between brother and sister. On this day, sister ties 'rakhi' on the wrist of brother to protect him from all evil influences and pray for his well-being and prosperity. In return, the brother promises to protect his sister under all circumstances.

8. **Dussehra:** It is a festival of celebrating Lord Rama's victory over the demon king 'Ravana'. On this day, huge effigies (statue) of Ravana, Kumbhakarna and Meghanada are burned. It is also known as Vijayadashami. It is celebrated on the tenth day of Navratri.

★ **National Festivals**

1. **Independence Day:** It is celebrated on 15th August every year. On 15 August, 1947, India got independence from British Rule. On the Independence Day, Prime Minister hoists National Flag and gives speech at the Red Fort in Delhi.

2. **Republic Day:** It is celebrated on 26th January every year. On 26 January, 1950, the Constitution of India came into force. The President of India raises the National Flag at Rajpath in New Delhi. It is followed by parades cultural programs.

3. **Gandhi Jayanti:** It is celebrated on 2nd October every year to honour the birthday of Mahatma Gandhi. His full name was Mohandas Karamchand Gandhi. People pay tribute by offering flowers on his Samadhi at Raj ghat in New Delhi.

Our Country and the World

★ **Famous Personalities**
1. **A. P. J. Abdul Kalam:** A. P. J. Abdul Kalam was the 11th president of India. He is also known as the 'Missile Man' of India. We all celebrate his birth anniversary as "World Students' Day".

2. **Mahatma Gandhi:** Mahatma Gandhi is popularly known as the Father of the Nation. He is also known as 'Bapu' or 'Gandhiji'. He was the pioneer of Indian Independence Movement against the British Rule.

3. **B. R. Ambedkar:** B. R. Ambedkar was the first Law Minister of India. He is known as the "Father of the Indian Constitution".

4. **Sachin Tendulkar:** Sachin Tendulkar is an Indian cricketer and is the highest run-scorer in Test cricket. He started playing cricket in international matches at the age of 16.

5. **Jawaharlal Nehru:** Jawaharlal Nehru was a political leader and a freedom fighter. He was the first Prime Minister of independent India. He is popularly known as 'Chacha Nehru' among children.

6. **Lata Mangeshkar:** Lata Mangeshkar is a magnificent playback singer and music director of India . She has sung over 50,000 songs in 20 Indian languages. She was awarded with the title "Daughter of The Nation" on her 90th birthday.

7. **Mary Kom:** Mary Kom is the first Indian female boxer who won gold medal in Asian Games.

DID YOU KNOW?

Taj Mahal was built by the great Mughal emperor Shah Jahan in the memory of his beloved wife Mumtaz Mahal. Around 22,000 artisans from across India, Iran, and Central Asia took 20 years to complete this architectural wonder.

★ **Famous Monuments**

Taj Mahal is located in Agra.

Our Country and the World

Red Fort is located in Delhi.

India Gate is located in Delhi.

Qutub Minar is located in Delhi.

> **DID YOU KNOW?**
> Qutub Minar has 379 stairs inside the Miner to reach the top.

Jama Masjid is located in Delhi.

Hawa Mahal is located in Jaipur.

Golden Temple is located in Amritsar.

> **DID YOU KNOW?**
> The Golden Temple is regarded as the most sacred place of worship for the Sikhs. The foundation of the Golden Temple was laid down by a Muslim saint Mian Mir.

Victoria Memorial is located in Kolkata.

Gol Gumbaz is located in Karnataka.

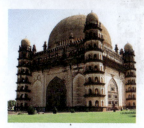

Charminar is Hyderabad.

Lotus Temple is located Delhi.

★ **Famous Dance Forms**

1. **Bharatanatyam** – Dance of Tamil Nadu.
2. **Kathakali** – Dance of Kerala.

3. **Kathak** – Dance of Uttar Pradesh.
4. **Manipuri** – Dance of Manipur.

5. **Kuchipudi** – Dance of Andhra Pradesh.
6. **Odissi** – Dance of Odisha.

Our Country and the World

★ **National Symbols**
1. **National Flag:** Tiranga, a rectangular flap consists of three colors -- saffron at top, white in the middle with Ashoka Chakra(blue) having 24 spokes at the center and green at the bottom.

2. **National Anthem:** 'Jana Gana Mana', was composed by Rabindranath Tagore.
3. **National Song:** Song 'Vande Mataram', was composed by Bankim Chandra Chatterjee.
4. **National River:** River Ganga' or 'Ganges', the longest river of India.
5. **National Emblem:** The Lion capital of Ashoka, having four lions sitting back to back, fourth one remains hidden.
6. **National Bird:** Peacock

7. **National Flower:** Lotus

8. **National Fruit:** Mango

9. **National Animal:** Tiger

10. **National Tree:** Banyan Tree

83

World

There are total 195 countries in the world and India is one of them.

★ **Flags**

Country	Flag
Afghanistan	
Australia	
Bangladesh	
Brazil	
Canada	
China	
France	

Our Country and the World

Country	Flag
India	
Japan	
Pakistan	
Russia	
Malaysia	
Sri Lanka	
United Kingdom	
United States of America	

★ Some Important Places

The Statue of Liberty – New York

The Eiffel Tower – Paris

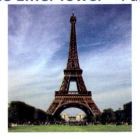

Sydney Opera House – Australia

Tower of Pisa – Italy

Big Ben – London

The Pyramids of Giza – Egypt

Golden Gate Bridge – San Francisco

Millennium Park – Chicago

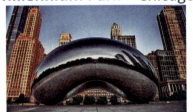

Walt Disney Concert Hall – Los Angeles

Great Wall of China – China

Our Country and the World

★ **Famous Personalities of the World**

1. **Albert Einstein:**
   - One of the greatest scientists of all time.
   - Worked in the field of science and technology.

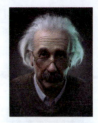

2. **Rabindranath Tagore:**
   - Worked in the field of music and literature.
   - Also known as Kabiguru.

3. **Sania Mirza:**
   - Famous tennis player of India.
   - First women to win Grand Slam Title.

4. **Barack Obama :**
   - 44th President of United States of America.
   - In 2009, he won Nobel Peace Prize.

5. **Kalpana Chawla:**
   - Astronaut and engineer who was one of the seven members of the crew that flew on the space shuttle Columbia in 1997.
   - First woman of Indian origin to go to space.

6. **Mother Teresa:**
   - Devoted her whole life to serve humanity.
   - Won Nobel Peace Prize in 1979.

★ **Some Important Days**

15th January	Army Day
26th January	Republic Day
28th February	National Science Day
3rd March	National Defence Day, World Wildlife Day

8th March	International Women's Day
22nd March	World Water Day
22nd April	Earth Day
5th June	World Environment Day
15th August	Independence Day
5th September	Teacher's Day
11th November	National Education Day
14th November	Children's Day

Multiple Choice Questions

LEVEL 1

1. Where are the Pyramids of Giza located?

   (a) Egypt (b) Mexico
   (c) Rome (d) China **[2019]**

2. Which of the following is NOT a national symbol of India?
   (a) Mango
   (b) Rose
   (c) The Ganga
   (d) Jana Gana Mana **[2019]**

3. The Statue of Liberty is located in _____.
   (a) New York City
   (b) France
   (c) Indonesia
   (d) London

   [2018]

4. Identify the famous personality shown in the picture.

   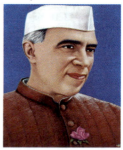

   (a) Rabindranath Tagore
   (b) Mahatma Gandhi
   (c) Jawaharlal Nehru
   (d) Subhash Chandra Bose

   [2018]

5. 'Millennium Park' is located in which country?
   (a) China
   (b) France
   (c) Italy
   (d) United States

   [2017]

6. Which of the following is known as the 'Festival of Brother and Sister'?
   (a) Diwali
   (b) Teacher's Day
   (c) Raksha Bandhan
   (d) Holi [2017]

7. It is the holiest Gurudwara of Sikhs:
   (a) Golden Temple
   (b) Lotus Temple
   (c) Sun Temple
   (d) None of these [2017]

8. *Gulal* and coloured water are used in which of the following festivals?
   (a) Holi
   (b) Diwali
   (c) Dussehra
   (d) Eid [2016]

9. Which of the following is the famous cricketer of India?
   (a)
   Sania Mirza
   (b)
   Sachin Tendulkar
   (c)
   Barack Obama
   (d)
   Albert Einstein [2016]

10. Which day is celebrated on 22nd April?
    (a) Women's Day
    (b) Navy Day
    (c) Republic Day
    (d) Earth Day [2016]

11. Italy is famous for:
    (a) Big Ben
    (b) Walt Disney concert hall
    (c) The Eiffel Tower
    (d) Tower of Pisa [2016]

12. Raj Ghat is the samadhi sthal of which of the following national leaders?

    (a)  (b)

    (c) (d)

    [2015]

13. Which of the following was a social worker who helped poor, old and sick people?

    (a)  (b)
    Sania Mirza   Mother Teresa

    (c) (d)
    Rabindranath   Barack
    Tagore   Obama

    [2015]

14. Who among the following worked in the field of science?
    (a) Rabindranath Tagore
    (b) Albert Einstein
    (c) APJ Abdul Kalam
    (d) Both (b) and (c) [2015]

15. How many spokes are there in the wheel of Indian National Flag?
    (a) 26   (b) 24
    (c) 30   (d) 32 [2015]

16. Identify the festival related to the picture shown.

    (a) Eid   (b) Christmas
    (c) Diwali   (d) Holi

17. Identify the shapes of the following in the National Flag of India.
    (i) Ashoka Chakra
    (ii) Green strip
    (a) (i) - Circle, (ii) - Rectangle
    (b) (i) - Square, (ii) - Square
    (c) (i) - Circle, (ii) - Square
    (d) (i) - Rectangle, (ii) – Circle

18. Which of the following is India's national Tree?
    (a) Mango tree
    (b) Banyan tree
    (c) Pine tree
    (d) Peepal tree

19. Which among the following is the National Bird of India?

    (a)    (b)

    (c)    (d)

20. Which of the following monuments is situated in Delhi?

    (a) 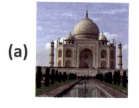   (b)

    (c) (image)   (d)

21. Match the following and select the correct option.

	State		Dance
1.	Kuchipudi	A.	Kerala
2.	Manipuri	B.	Andhra Pradesh
3.	Kathakali	C.	Manipur

    (a) 1-B, 2-C, 3-A
    (b) 1-C, 2-B, 3-A
    (c) 1-A, 2-B, 3-C
    (d) 1-B, 2-A, 3-C

22. Which of the following is a correct match?
  (a) Christmas – *Lakshmi Puja*
  (b) Eid – *Meethi Sevaiyaan*
  (c) Gurpurab – *Santa Claus*
  (d) Diwali – *Colours*

23. Teacher's Day is celebrated on ____.
  (a) 5th September
  (b) 2nd October
  (c) 14th November
  (d) 30th January

24. How many lions can one see in India's National Emblem?
  (a) 4   (b) 1
  (c) 3   (d) 2

25. Identify the given monument.

  (a) Gol Gumbaz   (b) Charminar
  (c) Hawa Mahal   (d) Red Fort

LEVEL 2

1. India has more than one name. It is also known as _____.
  (a) Hindustan   (b) Bengal
  (c) Utkal   (d) Banga **[2019]**

2. Some cities in India were earlier known by some other names. What is the old name of Chennai?
  (a) Cochin
  (b) Calcutta
  (c) Trivandrum
  (d) Madras   **[2018]**

3. Identify 'X' and 'Y'.

London	'X'
'Y'	Australia

  (a) X = Big Ben; Y = The Eiffel Tower
  (b) X = Millennium Park; Y = Big Ben
  (c) X = Big Ben; Y = Millennium Park
  (d) X = Big Ben; Y = Sydney Opera House   **[2017]**

4. Which one of the following is correctly matched?
  (a) Bangladesh –
  (b) Italy –
  (c) Pakistan –
  (d) Sri Lanka –
   [2017]

5. Which of the following is true about the given image?

  (a) It is the festival of colours.
  (b) People put gulal on one another.
  (c) People prepare Sevaiyaan.
  (d) Both (a) & (b)   **[2017]**

6. Who hoists the National Flag on Independence Day at the Red Fort?
   (a) President
   (b) Governor
   (c) Chief Minister
   (d) Prime Minister **[2016]**

7. Which one is MISMATCHED?
   (a) Sachin Tendulkar – Cricketer
   (b) Jawaharlal Nehru – First Prime Minister of India
   (c) Mahatma Gandhi – Father of the Nation
   (d) None of these **[2016]**

8. Who among the following is also known as 'Bapu'?

   (a)   (b)

   (c)   (d)

   [2015]

9. Which one of the following is ODD one?
   (a) Mahatma Gandhi
   (b) Jawaharlal Nehru
   (c) Narendra Modi
   (d) Barack Obama **[2015]**

10. National Anthem 'Jana Gana Mana' has been written by :
    (a) Bankim Chandra Chatterjee
    (b) Rabindranath Tagore
    (c) Jawaharlal Nehru
    (d) Sarojini Naidu

11. The beautiful monument, located in Agra, was built by Mughal emperor Shah Jahan. Identify this monument among the following.

    (a)

    (b)

    (c)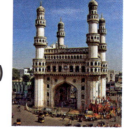

    (d)

12. Read the following statements and identify them as True or False.
    (1) On 15th August, India got independence.
    (2) The Prime Minister hoists National Flag at Red Fort in Delhi.
    (3) On Republic day, a parade is held in New Delhi on the Raj Ghat.
    (a) F,T,T   (b) T,T,F
    (c) T,F,T   (d) F,F,T

13. On which of the following occasion people clean and decorate their houses and burn crackers?
    (a) Eid
    (b) Christmas
    (c) Diwali
    (d) Holi
14. Which of the following festivals is celebrated on the same date every year?
    (a) Christmas
    (b) Diwali
    (c) Holi
    (d) Eid
15. Which of the following is an INCORRECT match?

Column I		Column II	
(a)	Holi	i.	Colours
(b)	Dussehra	ii.	Effigy of Ravana gets burnt
(c)	Diwali	iii.	*Meethi Sevaiyaan*
(d)	Christmas	iv.	Santa Claus

16. Which of the following statement is correct for dussehra?
    (a) It is celebrated on the tenth day of Navratri.
    (b) During this festival people to go to mosque for prayer.
    (c) It is the festival of colours.
    (d) It is the National Festival of India.
17. The beautiful temple shown in the picture is in New Delhi. It is open to people of all religions. What is it called?

    (a) Lotus Temple
    (b) Golden Temple
    (c) Charminar
    (b) Taj Mahal
18. Match Column I with Column II and select the correct option.

	Column I		Column II
A.	Strip on the top of India's National Flag	1.	White
B.	Strip in the center of India's National Flag	2.	Saffron
C.	Strip at the bottom of India's National Flag	3.	Blue
D.	Ashoka Chakra in the middle of India's National Flag	4.	Green

    (a) A-2, B-1, C-4, D-3
    (b) A-3, B-4, C-1, D-2
    (c) A-4, B-3, C-2, D-1
    (d) A-2, B-3, C-4, D-1
19. Which of the following festivals is also known as Vijayadashami?
    (a) Diwali
    (b) Raksha Bandhan
    (c) Holi
    (d) Dussehra

20. How many names of festivals are hidden in the following word grid?

C	H	R	I	S	T	M	A	S
X	D	I	W	L	I	H	E	T
T	W	E	I	D	G	A	J	C
N	Q	L	K	I	U	L	U	H
P	S	O	I	W	R	A	H	R
O	I	N	C	A	U	H	O	T
T	Z	M	S	L	B	Z	L	M
J	R	U	P	I	H	X	I	O
G	U	R	U	P	U	R	A	B

(a) 4   (b) 5
(c) 6   (d) 7

ACHIEVERS SECTION

1. Read the given statements and identify the monuments.
   A. This is located in Delhi and made up of red sandstone.
   B. This is located in Agra and is made up of marble.

	A	B
(a)	Gateway of India	Jama Masjid
(b)	Charminar	Qutub Minar
(c)	Red Fort	Taj Mahal
(d)	Lotus Temple	India Gate

   [2018]

2. Identify 'X', 'Y' and 'Z'.

'X'	Gulal	Coloured
Christmas	'Y'	Christmas Tree
National Festivals	Independence Day	'Z'

   (a) X = Holi, Y = Seviyan, Z = Eid
   (b) X = Holi, Y = Santa Claus, Z = Republic Day
   (c) X = Eid, Y = Holi, Z = Teacher's Day
   (d) X = Diwali, Y = Santa Claus, Z = Christmas Day **[2017]**

3. By identifying the festival being celebrated as shown in the given picture, tell how people celebrate this festival?

   (a) They decorate house with day lamps and flowers.
   (b) They go to mosque to pray Namaz.
   (c) They throw coloured water on one another.
   (d) They decorate Christmas tree.
   [2015]

4. Your friend Shiva does not know how Independence Day is celebrated. As a friend what you wil tell him about this National Festival?
   (a) On National days, we use to burn crackers.
   (b) On National days, we use to play with colors.

(c) On this day, India got independence so our Prime Minister hoists National Flag at the Red Fort.
(d) On this day, we go to temple and do prayer. **[2015]**

5. Consider the following statements and choose the correct option.
   Statement A: Eid is a national festival.
   Statement B: Eid is celebrated mostly by Muslims.
   (a) Statement A is true and Statement B is False.
   (b) Statement A is false and Statement B is True.
   (c) Both the statements are true.
   (d) Both the statements are false.

Answer-Key

LEVEL 1

1. (a)	2. (b)	3. (a)	4. (c)	5. (d)
6. (c)	7. (a)	8. (a)	9. (b)	10. (d)
11. (d)	12. (a)	13. (b)	14. (d)	15. (b)
16. (b)	17. (a)	18. (b)	19. (d)	20. (b)
21. (a)	22. (b)	23. (a)	24. (c)	25. (a)

LEVEL 2

1. (a)	2. (d)	3. (d)	4. (a)	5. (d)
6. (d)	7. (d)	8. (b)	9. (d)	10. (b)
11. (b)	12. (b)	13. (c)	14. (a)	15. (c)
16. (a)	17. (a)	18. (a)	19. (d)	20. (b)

ACHIEVERS SECTION

1. (c)	2. (b)	3. (b)	4. (c)	5. (b)

Answers with Explanations

LEVEL 1

2. **Correct option is (b)**
   Explanation: Mango is our National fruit. The Ganga is our National river. Song 'Jana Gana Mana' is our National anthem. Lotus is our National flower.

4. **Correct option is (c)**
   Explanation: Jawaharlal Nehru was an eminent leader of the Indian Independence struggle. He was the first Prime Minister of India.

6. **Correct option is (c)**
   Explanation: Raksha Bandhan is known as the 'Festival of Brother and Sister' as sister ties 'rakhi' on the wrist of brother as a symbol of her love for her brother and prays for his well-being and prosperity. In return the brother promises to protect her under all circumstances.

7. **Correct option is (a)**
   Explanation: Golden Temple in Amritsar is considered as the holiest Gurudwara of Sikhs. It was founded by the forth Sikh Guru, Guru Ram Das.

8. **Correct option is (a)**
   Explanation: Holi is the festival of colours. People play Holi by putting gulal and throwing coloured water on one another.

9. **Correct option is (b)**
   Explanation: Sachin Tendulkar is the famous cricketer of India. He is one of the greatest batsmen of all times.

10. **Correct option is (d)**
    Explanation: Earth Day is celebrated on 22nd April every year worldwide to demonstrate the support towards environment.

11. **Correct option is (d)**
    Explanation: Tower of Pisa is a bell tower located in Italy. It is famous because it is not vertical, it is leaning.

12. **Correct option is (a)**
    Explanation: Raj Ghat is a black marble memorial dedicated to Mahatma Gandhi.

13. **Correct option is (b)**
    Explanation: Mother Teresa devoted her whole life to serve humanity.

14. **Correct option is (d)**
    Explanation: Albert Einstein was a German mathematician and physicist and APJ Abdul Kalam was an Indian aerospace scientist.

15. **Correct option is (b)**
    Explanation: There are 24 spokes in the Wheel, Ashoka Chakra, of the Indian National Flag.

16. **Correct option is (b)**
    Explanation: Festival related to picture is Christmas. People wear new clothes, decorate Christmas tree, exchange gifts and eat festive meals on Christmas.

17. **Correct option is (a)**
    Explanation: National flag of India has three rectangular stripes, Saffron, White and Green. It also

Our Country and the World

has a circular wheel in the center, known as the Ashoka Chakra.

18. Correct option is (b)

    Explanation: Banyan tree is the National tree of India.

19. Correct option is (d)

    Explanation: Peacock is the National bird of India.

20. Correct option is (b)

    Explanation:
    (a) Taj Mahal – Agra
    (b) India Gate – Delhi
    (c) Charminar – Hyderabad
    (d) Hawa Mahal – Jaipur

21. Correct option is (a)

    Explanation:

State	Dance
Kuchipudi	Andhra Pradesh
Manipuri	Manipur
Kathakali	Kerala

22. Correct option is (b)

    Explanation: Every festival has one signature dish and *meethi sevaiyaan* is special dish for Eid.

23. Correct option is (a)

    Explanation: In India, Teacher's Day is celebrated on 5th September every year to honor the contribution made by teachers to the society as it is the birth anniversary of the great teacher Dr. Sarvepalli Radhakrishnan.

24. Correct option is (c)

    Explanation: One can see only 3 lions in India's National Emblem, forth one is hidden from the view.

LEVEL 2

1. Correct option is (a)

    Explanation: India is also known as Hindustan and Bharat.

3. Correct option is (d)

    Explanation:

London	Big Ben
Australia	Sydney Opera House

4. Correct option is (a)

    Explanation:

5. Correct option is (d)

Explanation: The given image shows a scene of Holy. Holi is the festival of colours and people play Holi by putting gulal and coloured water on one another.

7. Correct option is (d)

Explanation: All options are correct as Sachin Tendulkar is a famous Indian cricketer, Jawaharlal Nehru was the first Prime Minister of India and Mahatma Gandhi is also known as the Father of the Nation.

8. Correct option is (b)

Explanation: Mahatma Gandhi is also known as Bapu.

11. Correct option is (b)

Explanation: Taj Mahal was built by the great Mughal emperor Shah Jahan in the memory of his beloved wife Mumtaz Mahal.

13. Correct option is (c)

Explanation: On Diwali, people clean and decorate their houses with clay lamps and candles. Children burn crackers during this festival.

14. Correct option is (a)

Explanation: Among the given festivals, Christmas is the only festival which is celebrated on the same date every year which is 25th December as the birth anniversary of Jesus Christ.

15. Correct option is (c)

Explanation: 'Meethi sevaiyaan' is a special dish, prepared in Eid.

17. Correct option is (a)

Explanation: The image shown in the given picture is of Lotus Temple. It is a Bahai Tample, here people from all religions are allowed to visit.

18. Correct option is (a)

Explanation: National Flag of India consists of three colors— saffron at the top, white in the middle and green at the bottom and Ashok Chakra (blue) at the centre.

19. Correct option is (d)

Explanation: Dussehra is also known as Vijayadashami, as it symbolizes victory of good over evil and celebrated on the tenth day (dashmi) of navratri.

20. Correct option is (b)

Explanation: Holi, Diwali, Christmas, Gurupurab, Eid.

ACHIEVERS SECTION

2. Correct option is (b)

Explanation: Holi is played with gulal and coloured water. Children believe that Santa Claus brings gifts for them on Christmas and they also decorate Christmas trees. Independence Day and Republic Day are National Festival of India.

3. Correct option is (b)

Explanation: Festival shown in picture is Eid. People go to mosque to pray Namaaz on this day.

Our Country and the World

4. **Correct option is (c)**
   Explanation: On Independence Day, India got independence. On this day, Prime Minister hoists National Flag at the Red Fort.

5. **Correct option is (b)**
   Explanation: National Festivals of India are Independence Day, Republic Day and Gandhi Jayanti. Eid is a religious festival which is celebrated mostly by followers of Islam, *i.e.* Muslims.

How to make learning
Fun, Effective & Responsive
at the same time?

It's easy!
Scan the QR codes below

Festivals of India　　**Monuments of India**　　**Our Country**

and get started!

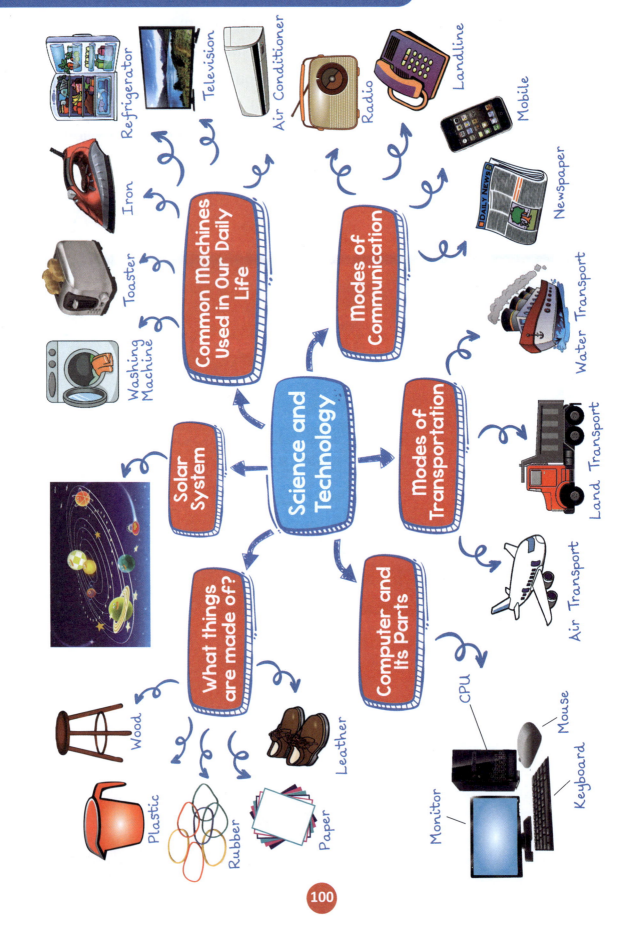

CHAPTER 5: SCIENCE AND TECHNOLOGY

Learning Outcomes

Children would be able to :
- Know the difference between humans and machines;
- Identify common machines used in everyday life;
- Identify and spell various parts of computer;
- Know various parts of our universe;
- List out the planets in the Solar System.

Concept Review

INTRODUCTION

Science is present everywhere around us. It plays a significant role in our life. In our everyday life, we use various types of machines that perform various tasks. These machines have become a very important part of our lives and they help us in many ways. This chapter makes children aware about the application of science in our day-to-day life.

★ **Difference between Humans and Machines**

Humans	Machines
Humans have feelings and emotions and they can express them.	Machines do not have feelings or emotions.
Humans behave according to the situations.	Machines do not have a capability to understand different situations.
Humans behave as per their consciousness.	Machines do not have thinking of their own; they work as per the given instructions.

Solar System

Solar System consists of eight Planets. Sun is at the center of the Solar System. All eight planets revolve around the Sun.

DID YOU KNOW?

Mercury is the closest planet to the Sun. Jupiter is the largest planet of the Solar System. Neptune is the farthest planet from the Sun.

★ **Sun**
- The Sun is round in shape.
- It is too hot as it is a big ball of burning gases.
- The Sun rises in the east in the morning and sets in the West in the evening.
- The Sun is the source of heat and light on earth.

AMAZING FACT

The Sun is the star closest star to our Earth.

★ **Moon**
- The Moon is smaller than the Earth and is closer to Earth than the Sun.
- The Moon does not have its own light, its surface reflects the light received from the Sun.
- There is no life on Moon due to absence of water and air.
- The Moon is not hot like the Sun.

Science and Technology

★ **Stars**
- Stars appear very small to us as they are very far from us.
- The stars have their own light. Some stars are as bright as or even brighter than the Sun.

★ **Clouds**
- Clouds are made up of water vapour.
- They appear white in colour most of the time.
- When it is about to rain, the clouds appear dark grey in color.

★ **Rainbow**
- Rainbow is a seven coloured arc shaped band that we see in the sky sometimes after the rain. It appears in the sky when sunlight enters water droplets. It has seven colours – violet, indigo, blue, green, yellow, orange and red.

 Common Machines Used in Daily Life

With the advancement of science and technology, we now have various machines that make our life easy, comfortable and better.

1. **Television:** It is a device used to watch different shows news, sports, etc., for entertainment. It also boosts our knowledge.

2. **Air Conditioner:** It is a machine that keeps our house cool by drawing out heat from inside the house.

3. **Washing Machine:** It is a machine used to wash laundry.

4. **Refrigerator:** It is a machine used to keep our food and drinks cool and fresh for longer period of time.

DID YOU KNOW?

Refrigerator is more efficient when it has more items in it. You should not put hot or warm food inside the refrigerator. Let it cool first and then put it inside.

5. **Iron:** It is used to remove wrinkles from our clothes.

Science and Technology

6. **Vacuum Cleaner:** It is used to clean our house, bed, sofa, carpet, floor, etc., as it sucks up all the dust and dirt from them.

7. **Computer:** It is a device used to perform various tasks such as doing official work, calculations, writing letters, playing games, watching movies, etc.

 Parts of Computer

1. **Monitor:** It looks like a television. It displays all the work which is going on inside the computer. It is an output device.

2. **Keyboard:** It has various small buttons which are known as keys. It is an input device. It is used to for typing.

3. **CPU (Central Processing Unit):** It stores all the information and is known as the 'Brain of the Computer'.

4. **Mouse:** It is a pointing device which is used to control the movement of the pointer on the computer screen. It is used to point and select items on computer screen, playing games, making drawings, etc. It is also an input device.

DID YOU KNOW?

Mobile phones work through radio waves it is harmful for human being.

Modes of Communication

Communication is conveying a message to someone. Modes of communication are used to communicate.

 ## Means of Transportation

Transportation means carrying people and goods from one place to another. There are various modes of transportation that are land, water and in air. Ship is a means of water transport, aeroplane is a means of air transport and bus and train are means of land transport.

Science and Technology

What are Things Made of?

A material is what an object is made of. There are different materials from which various objects used in our day to day life are made.

1. **Wood :** It is a hard and fibrous material forming most of the branches and trunk of trees. We use various products made up of wood in our daily life such as table, chair, bed, almirah, etc.

2. **Paper:** It is a thin sheet material obtained from plants, mainly used for writing, packing, printing, drawing, etc. Paper is used for making shopping bag. Books are also made up of paper.

3. **Rubber:** It is a natural product, obtained from latex, a milky liquid present in the cells of rubber-producing plants. We use various products made up of rubber in our daily life such as toys, tyres, slippers, etc.

4. **Plastic:** It is synthetic or material that can be made from various chemical substance. There are various products which are made up of plastic such as mugs, bottles, toys, pipes, carry bags, etc.

5. **Cotton:** It is a natural, soft and fluffy staple fiber that is obtained from the seedpod also known as cotton ball of the cotton plant. It is used to make different types of clothes.

6. **Leather:** It made from the skin of animal. This material is mainly used to make shoes, bags, belt, jackets, etc.

Science in Everyday Life

Science is involved in playing, cooking, eating, driving, breathing, etc. Examples of use of science in our daily life are:

★ We go from one place to another with the help of bike, car, train, etc. These all are inventions of science.

★ The house is a product of science in which we live.

★ We use gas stove, microwave, toaster, etc., in our kitchen. These all are inventions of science.

★ We use soap, shampoo, oil, talcum powder, etc. These all are result of science.

★ Torch, candle, lamps, etc., we use as a source of light are also products of science.

★ The clothes, we wear are given by science to us.

★ Iron that we use to remove wrinkles from our clothes is also an invention of science.

★ Electricity, through which machines and devices such as refrigerator, computer, television, iron, washing machine, etc., run are also inventions of science.

Life cannot be imagined without any of these, as they have become a necessity in our lives.

Science and Technology

Multiple Choice Questions

LEVEL 1

1. Which of the following is an input device?

   (a)   (b)

   (c)   (d) All of these

   [2019]

2. Which of the following is not a source of light?
   (a) Window pane
   (b) Sun
   (c) Torch
   (d) Candle   [2019]

3. Which of the following letters will complete the given name of the machine used in the kitchen?

   T_ _ST_R

   (a) ASE   (b) OAE
   (b) MUM   (d) LAN   [2019]

4. Which of the following machines can be used to play music?

   (a)   (b)

   (c)   (d)

   [2018]

5. How many colours are there in a rainbow?
   (a) 6   (b) 7
   (c) 8   (d) 9   [2015]

6. Humans have:
   (a) Consciousness
   (b) Feelings
   (c) Emotions
   (d) All the above   [2015]

7. The object shown in the picture is a commonly used machine. What is it?

   (a) Refrigerator
   (b) Washing machine
   (c) Toaster
   (d) Iron

8. Identify the given part of a computer.

   (a) Monitor   (b) Mouse
   (c) Keyboard   (d) CPU

9. What is at the center of our Solar System?
   (a) Sun   (d) Moon
   (c) Earth   (d) Venus

10. Which is the third planet from the Sun?
(a) Mercury (b) Earth
(c) Venus (d) Jupiter

11. Which is the closest planet to the Sun?
(a) Earth (b) Venus
(c) Neptune (d) Mercury

12. How many planets are there in our Solar System?
(a) 5 (b) 7
(c) 8 (d) 9

13. Which of the following is a means of communication?

(a) (b)

(c) (d) All of the above

14. Which of the following is a means of transportation?

(a) (b)

(c) (d)

15. Match the columns and select the correct option.

Column I		Column II	
A.	(monitor)	1.	Keyboard
B.	(mouse)	2.	Monitor
C.	(keyboard)	3.	CPU
D.	(CPU tower)	4.	Mouse

(a) A-1, B-4, C-2, D-3
(b) A-2, B-4, C-1, D-3
(c) A-4, B-3, C-2, D-1
(d) A-4, B-2, C-3, D-1

16. The Sun rises in the _____ and sets in the _____.
(a) West, East
(b) West, North
(c) East, West
(d) North, West

17. The pencil is made up of _____.
(a) Plastic
(b) Wood
(c) Rubber
(d) Leather

18. The given pencil box is made up of _____.

(a) Plastic
(b) Wood
(c) Rubber
(d) Leather

19. Unscramble the gives letters and select the correct option.

    NREPWSPAE
    (a) New Paper
    (b) Newspaper
    (c) Sewpaper
    (d) Papersnew

20. Identify the mode of communication shown in the given picture.

    (a) Television (b) Radio
    (c) Telephone   (d) Letter

21. The Sun is a _____ ball of fire.
    (a) Hot   (b) Small
    (c) Cool   (d) Ring

22. The Sun gives us _____ and light.
    (a) Heat
    (b) Air
    (c) Water
    (d) All of the above

23. Which of the following can be done _____ on a computer?
    (a) Games
    (b) Sending Email
    (c) Watching movies
    (d) All of the above

24. Machines make our work _____.
    (a) Easy
    (b) Difficult
    (c) Complex
    (d) All of the above

25. Rearrange the given letters to get the name of the following computer part.

    TOMIRON

    (a) TORMION   (b) MONITOR
    (c) TORMINO   (d) IRONTOM

LEVEL 2

1. Which of the following runs on electricity?
   (a) Bicycle
   (b) Bullock-cart
   (c) Refrigerator
   (d) Bus   **[2018]**

2. Which of the following statements is INCORRECT?
   (a) Moon is a satellite of the Earth.
   (b) The Sun is the nearest star to the Earth.
   (c) Planets give out their own light.
   (d) There are eight planets in the solar system.   **[2018]**

3. **Statement A :** Humans behave according to work.
   Statement B : Machines just perform as they are taught.
   (a) Statement A is correct.
   (b) Statement B is correct.
   (c) Both are correct.
   (d) None of these [2017]

4. Which one keeps our food fresh for longer?
   (a) Phone
   (b) Refrigerator
   (c) Washing machine
   (d) None of these [2016]

5. Which of the following parts of computer, store all the data?

   (a)  (b)

   (c)  (d)

6. Which of the following is made up of rubber?
   (a) Tyre (b) Shirt
   (c) Book (d) Mobile phone

7. Look at the picture. What is this item made up of?
   (a) Leather
   (b) Cloth
   (c) Rubber
   (d) Plastic

8. Select the odd one out.
   (a) Iron
   (b) Refrigerator
   (c) Television
   (d) Chair

9. Which of the following is known as brain of computer?

   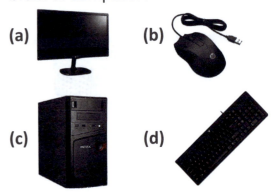

10. Look at the given pictures carefully and select the odd one out.

    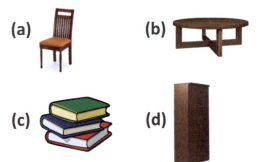

11. Which of the following is made up of paper?

12. State whether following statements are true or false.
    1. The sun is a star too.
    2. Moon supports life.
    3. Sun is a small ball of burning gases.
    4. Stars have their own light.
    (a) T, F, F, T   (b) T, T, F, T
    (c) T, F, F, F   (d) F, F, F, T

13. Match the columns and select the correct option.

Column I		Column II
A.	Sun	1. Moves around the earth
B.	Moon	2. Contain water vapour
C.	Earth	3. Nearest star to the earth
D.	Clouds	4. A beautiful planet

    (a) A-3, B-1, C-4, D-2
    (b) A-2, B-3, C-4, D-1
    (c) A-1, B-2, C-4, D-3
    (d) A-3, B-4, C-1, D-2

14. Match the columns and select the correct option.

Column I		Column II
A.	Uranus	1. Comes after Earth
B.	Mars	2. Comes after Mercury
C.	Venus	3. Comes after Saturn

    (a) A-2, B-1, C-3
    (b) A-3, B-1, C-2
    (c) A-1, B-3, C-2
    (d) A-3, B-2, C-1

15. Select the odd one out.

    (a)    (b)

    (c) 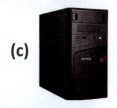   (d)

ACHIEVERS SECTION

1. Unscramble the jumbled letters given in Column I and match them with their images given in Column II.

Column I		Column II
A.	MNITORO	1. (camera image)
B.	DGII CMA	2. (monitor image)
C.	BWE CMA	3. (webcam image)

    (a) A-2, B-1, C-3   (b) A-1, B-3, C-2
    (c) A-3, B-2, C-1   (d) A-1, B-2, C-3

[2018]

2. The Earth is a _____ while the Moon is a _____.
   (a) Planet, Satellite
   (b) Satellite, Planet
   (c) Star, Planet
   (d) Planet, Star

3. How many names of planets are hidden in the given word grid?

T	M	M	K	S	C	S	U
U	E	A	R	T	H	O	N
D	R	R	T	A	V	L	I
S	C	S	P	R	Z	S	V
W	U	T	V	E	N	U	S
U	R	A	N	O	P	N	Q
M	Y	R	S	N	O	O	R
J	U	P	I	T	E	R	W

   (a) 4
   (b) 5
   (c) 6
   (d) 7

4. Identify 'X' and 'Y'.

It sucks dust and dirt.	'X'
'Y'	It removes wrinkles from clothes.

   (a) X – Vacuum cleaner, Y – Iron
   (b) X – Washing machine, Y – Iron
   (c) X – Vacuum cleaner, Y- Television
   (d) None of the above

5. Which of the following machines does NOT need electricity to run?
   (a) Washing machine
   (b) Vacuum cleaner
   (c) Bike
   (d) Computer

Answer-Key

LEVEL 1

1. (b)	2. (a)	3. (b)	4. (c)	5. (b)
6. (d)	7. (b)	8. (c)	9. (a)	10. (b)
11. (d)	12. (c)	13. (d)	14. (a)	15. (b)
16. (c)	17. (b)	18. (a)	19. (b)	20. (b)
21. (a)	22. (a)	23. (d)	24. (a)	25. (b)

LEVEL 2

1. (c)	2. (c)	3. (c)	4. (b)	5. (c)
6. (a)	7. (d)	8. (d)	9. (c)	10. (c)
11. (b)	12. (a)	13. (a)	14. (b)	15. (d)

Science and Technology

ACHIEVERS SECTION

| 1. (a) | 2. (a) | 3. (b) | 4. (a) | 5. (c) |

 ## Answers with Explanations

LEVEL 1

1. **Correct option is (b)**
   Explanation: Mouse is an input device as it is used to select data and send command to computer.

3. **Correct option is (b)**
   Explanation: Toaster is a small machine used to toast the slices of bread.

4. **Correct option is (c)**
   Explanation: Microwave is used to heat or cook food. Washing machine is used to wash laundry. Computer is used to play games, listen to music, news. Toaster is used to toast the slices of bread.

5. **Correct option is (b)**
   Explanation: There are seven colours in a rainbow, that are violet, indigo, blue, green, yellow, orange and red.

8. **Correct option is (c)**
   Explanation: The given part is a keyboard. It is a input device.

9. **Correct option is (a)**
   Explanation: Sun is at the center of the Solar System and all planets revolve around the Sun.

10. **Correct option is (b)**

Explanation: Planets in the order of their distance from the Sun is as follows:
Mercury, Venus, Earth (3rd planet), Mars, Jupiter, Saturn, Uranus, Neptune.

12. **Correct option is (c)**
    Explanation: There are eight planets in our Solar System, *viz.*, Mercury, Venus, Earth, Mars, Jupiter, Saturn, Uranus and Neptune.

14. **Correct option is (a)**
    Explanation: Train is a means of land transport through which people and goods are carried from one place to another.

16. **Correct option is (c)**
    Explanation: The Sun rises in the East and sets in the West. It is a universal fact.

19. **Correct option is (b)**
    Explanation: Newspaper is a means of communication.

20. **Correct option is (b)**
    Explanation: Radio is a means of communication through which a message can be send to a large number of people at a time.

115

21. **Correct option is (a)**
    Explanation: The sun is a hot ball of burning gases.
22. **Correct option is (a)**
    Explanation: The Sun gives us heat and light. In the absence of Sun, Earth would be a lifeless ball of ice-coated rock.
23. **Correct option is (d)**
    Explanation: We can play games on a computer send email and watch movies.
24. **Correct option is (a)**
    Explanation: Machines make our work easy as they take less time to do it and reduce human efforts.
25. **Correct option is (b)**
    Explanation: Monitor looks like a television. It displays all the information in the form of text and picture.

LEVEL 2

2. **Correct option is (c)**
    Explanation: Planets do not have their own light. They get light from the Sun.
3. **Correct option is (c)**
    Explanation: Humans have capability of understanding the situation and behave accordingly whereas machines do not have such capability.
4. **Correct option is (b)**
    Explanation: It is a machine used to keep our food and drinks cool and fresh for a longer period time.
5. **Correct option is (c)**
    Explanation: CPU stores all the data entered into the computer.
6. **Correct option is (a)**
    Explanation: Tyres of vehicles are made up of rubber. Shirt is made of cotton. Book is made up of paper. Body of mobile phone is made up of metal or plastic.
7. **Correct option is (d)**
    Explanation: The given picture is of a water bottle. It is made up of plastic.
8. **Correct option is (d)**
    Explanation: Except chair all others are machines.
9. **Correct option is (c)**
    Explanation: CPU is considered as the brain of computer as it stores all the data.
10. **Correct option is (c)**
    Explanation: Chair, table, and almirah are made of wood whereas, books are made of paper.
11. **Correct option is (b)**
    Explanation: Carry bags can be made up of paper also. They are recyclable.
12. **Correct option is (a)**
    Explanation: Moon does not support life. Sun is a big ball of burning gases.

Science and Technology

14. **Correct option is (b)**
 Explanation: Planets in order of distance from the Sun are: Mercury, Venus, Earth, Mars, Jupiter, Saturn, Uranus and Neptune.
15. **Correct option is (d)**
 Explanation: Except refrigerator, all other are parts of the computer.

ACHIEVERS SECTION

1. **Correct option is (a)**
 Explanation: **A**– Monitor
   B– DIGI CAM
   C– WEB CAM
2. **Correct option is (a)**
 Explanation: The Earth is a planet while the Moon is a satellite.
3. **Correct option is (b)**
 Explanation: Mercury, Mars, Earth, Venus and Jupiter
4. **Correct option is (a)**
 Explanation: Vacuum cleaner is used to clean the house as it sucks dust and dirt.
 Iron is used to remove wrinkles from clothes.
5. **Correct option is (c)**
 Explanation: Washing machine, vacuum cleaner and computer need electricity to run, whereas a bike needs battery or petrol as fuel.

How to make learning
Fun, Effective & Responsive
at the same time?

It's easy!
Scan the QR codes below

Machine Means of Communication Solar System

and get started!

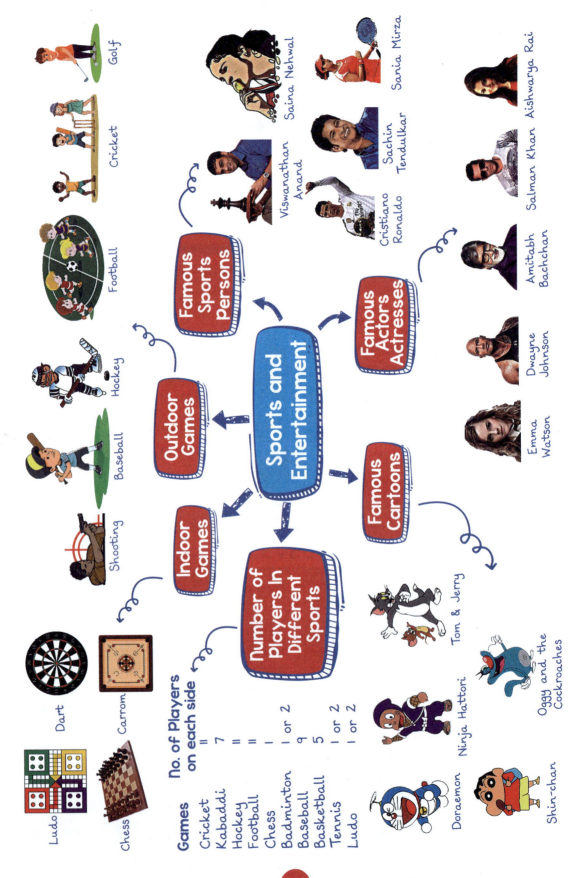

CHAPTER 6: SPORTS AND ENTERTAINMENT

Learning Outcomes

Children would be able to:
- Identify and differentiate indoor and outdoor games;
- Know the number of players in different games;
- Recognize famous sports personalities;
- Identify different sports field and equipment used for different sports.

Concept Review

INTRODUCTION

For growth and development of a child, it is important to play different types of games. This chapter makes students aware about various types of games which they can play, with friends, at school in park, at home, etc.

★ **Outdoor Games**

Outdoor games are those which we play outside the house. For example, cricket, football, badminton, hockey, basketball, etc. Net is used in some games to separate the players of different teams. For Example, tennis, badminton, volleyball, etc.

Tennis

Basketball

FUN TRIVIA

Baseball umpires are required to wear black underwear while on the job in case they split their pants.

Volleyball   Baseball

Hockey   Football

DID YOU KNOW?

Chess was originally named "Chaturanga" or "Chaturaangam" meaning intelligent or smart.

★ **Indoor Games**

Indoor games are those which we play inside the house. For example, chess, ludo, snake & ladder, carrom, video games, etc.

Ludo   Snake & Ladder   Chess   Carrom Board

★ **Number of Players in Some Famous Games**

Games	No. of Players on Each Side
Cricket	11
Kabaddi	7
Hockey	11
Football	11
Chess	1
Badminton	1 or 2
Baseball	9
Basketball	5
Tennis	1 or 2
Ludo	1 or 2

DID YOU KNOW?

Sachin Tendulkar is a famous cricketer who is also known as Master Blaster of Indian Cricket Team.
Milkha Singh is a famous track running who also known as the Flying Sikh in the whole world today.

Sports and Entertainment

★ **Famous Sports Personalities of India**

Name	Related Sport	Photograph
Sachin Tendulkar	Cricket	
Milkha Singh	Running	
Mahendra Singh Dhoni	Cricket	
Viswanathan Anand	Chess	
Mahesh Bhupathi	Tennis	
Sania Mirza	Tennis	
Saina Nehwal	Badminton	

MC Mary Kom	Boxing	
P. V. Sindhu	Badminton	

★ **Famous Sports Personalities of World**

Sports Person	Name	Related Sport
	Cristiano Ronaldo	Football Soccer
	Lionel Messi	Football Soccer
	Roger Federer	Tennis
	Novak Djokovic	Tennis
	Rafael Nadal	Tennis

DID YOU KNOW?

Cricket has an extensive number of terms associated with, it such as googly, no ball, LBW (leg before wicket), boundary, etc.

Sports and Entertainment

	Usain Bolt	Runner
	Serena Williams	Tennis

★ **Sport Field and Equipments**

Sport	Field/Court/Rink	Clothing/Equipments
Ice hockey		
Boxing		
Cricket		
Hockey		

123

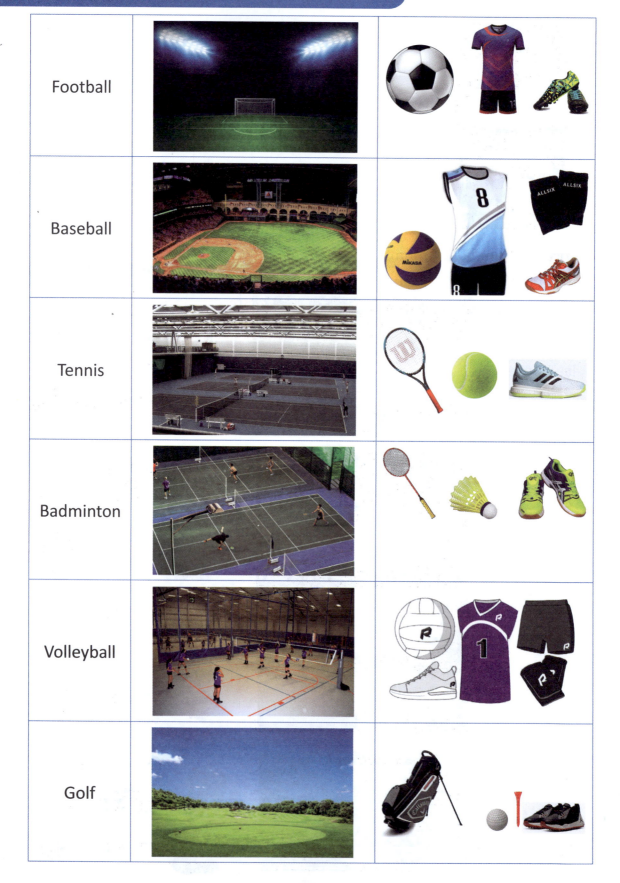

Sports and Entertainment

Basketball		
Swimming		
Skiing		

★ Famous Actors and Actresses

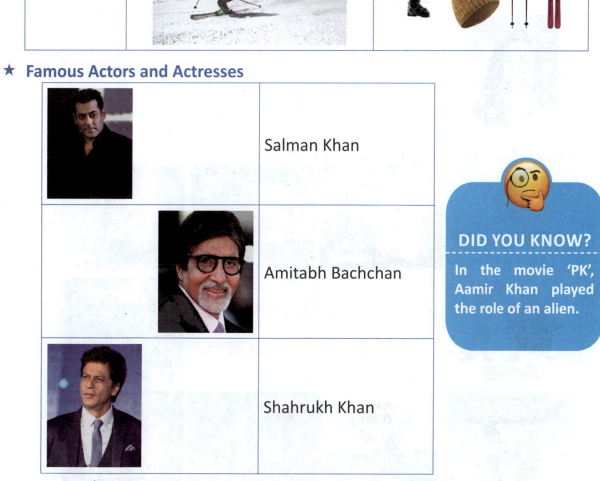

	Salman Khan
	Amitabh Bachchan
	Shahrukh Khan

DID YOU KNOW?

In the movie 'PK', Aamir Khan played the role of an alien.

	Dwayne Johnson	
	Leonardo DiCaprio	
	Emma Watson	
	Aishwarya Rai	

★ **Famous Cartoons and Their Main Characters**

 **Famous Cartooons and Their Main Characters**

  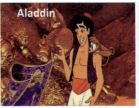 

Sports and Entertainment

Multiple Choice Questions

LEVEL 1

1. The character shown in the picture appears in the animated movie ____.

   (a) Frozen   (b) Zootopia
   (c) Aladdin   (d) Shrek   **[2019]**

2. For which sport would you wear this?

   (a) Swimming
   (b) Basketball
   (c) Roller skating
   (d) Tennis   **[2019]**

3. Look at the picture. Which sport is this?

   (a) Swimming   (b) Roller skating
   (c) Skiing   (d) Ice hockey
                                    [2019]

4. Identify the famous bollywood actor shown in the picture.

   (a) Salman Khan
   (b) Akshay Kumar
   (c) Shah Rukh Khan
   (d) Aamir Khan   **[2019]**

5. Name the cartoon characters shown in the given picture.

   (a) Wallace and Gromit
   (b) Tom and Jerry
   (c) Motu and Patlu
   (d) Timon & Pumbaa   **[2018]**

6. Identify the famous Bollywood actor shown in the picture.

   (a) Shah Rukh Khan
   (b) Amitabh Bachchan
   (c) Salman Khan
   (d) Amir Khan   **[2018]**

7. To which game is the sportswoman shown in the picture related?

(a) Tennis (b) Skating
(c) Table Tennis (d) Basketball

[2018]

8. To which game is the sportswoman shown in the picture related?

(a) Badminton (b) Lawn Tennis
(c) Boxing (d) Wrestling

[2017]

9. How many players are there in each side of Kabaddi game?
(a) 7 (b) 6
(c) 8 (d) 10 [2015]

10. Match the columns and select the correct option.

Column I (Games)		Column II (Number of Players)
A. Cricket	1.	5
B. Basketball	2.	9
C. Baseball	3.	1
D. Chess	4.	11

(a) A-4, B-1, C-2, D-3
(b) A-2, B-1, C-4, D-3
(c) A-1, B-4, C-2, D-3
(d) A-4, B-2, C-3, D-1

11. How many squares are there in chess board?
(a) 55 (b) 64
(c) 81 (d) 72

12. Which game is being played in the picture?

(a) Hockey (b) Football
(c) Cricket (d) Tennis

13. For which sport would you use these?

(a) Boxing (b) Tennis
(c) Hockey (d) Volleyball

14. Which of the following balls is used in the sport of basketball?

(a)

(b)

(c)

(d) None of the above

15. In which sport are the equipment shown in the picture used?

Sports and Entertainment

(a) Hockey (b) Football
(c) Cricket (d) Baseball

16. Which of the following is an indoor game?
    (a) Baseball (b) Golf
    (c) Chess (d) Rugby

17. Identify the sportsperson shown in the picture.

(a) Novak Djokovic
(b) Viswanathan Anand
(c) Mahesh Bhupathi
(d) Milkha Singh

18. Lionel Messi is famous for _____.
    (a) Soccer (b) Cricket
    (c) Hockey (d) Chess

19. Which of the following is an outdoor game?
    (a) Ludo
    (b) Chess
    (c) Hockey
    (d) Carrom

20. Identify the sportsperson shown in the given picture.

(a) Serena Williams
(b) Mary Kom
(c) Saina Nehwal
(d) Maria Sharapova

21. Match the columns and select the correct option.

Column I		Column II
A.	Cricket	1.
B.	Table Tennis	2.
C.	Ludo	3.
D.	Football	4.

(a) A-3, B-4, C-2, D-1
(b) A-4, B-3, C-1, D-2
(c) A-4, B-3, C-2, D-1
(d) A-2, B-3, C-1, D-4

22. Which sports is represented in the given image?

    (a) Tennis (b) Badminton
    (c) Ice hockey (d) Baseball

23. _____ are played in open area.
    (a) Indoor games
    (b) Outdoor games
    (c) Open games
    (d) Close games

24. Games we play under the covered area are:
    (a) Indoor games
    (b) Outdoor games
    (c) Open games
    (d) Close games

25. Which of these sports does NOT use net?
    (a) Badminton (b) Volleyball
    (c) Tennis (d) Baseball

LEVEL 2

1. In which of the following sports a ball is not used for playing?
   (a) Cricket (b) Snooker
   (c) Hockey (d) Badminton
   [2019]

2. In which game the term 'Leg Before Wicket (LBW)' is used?
   (a) Tennis (b) Cricket
   (c) Hockey (d) Basketball
   [2019]

3. Game played with curved sticks and a ball is _____.
   (a) Football (b) Basketball
   (c) Hockey (d) Volleyball
   [2017]

4. Choose the odd one:
   (a) Cricket
   (b) Football
   (c) Hockey
   (d) Snake & Ladder
   [2016]

5. The bat and ball game played between two teams of 11 players each on a roughly circular field is:
   (a) football
   (b) cricket
   (c) hockey
   (d) polo **[2015]**

6. Which of the following sports persons is called the Master Blaster?
   (a)
   (b)
   (c)
   (d)

7. Match the columns and select the correct option.

	Column I		Column II
A.	Cricket	1.	(shuttlecock)
B.	Hockey	2.	(cricket bat)
C.	Badminton	3.	(hockey stick)

(a) A-2, B-3, C-1 (b) A-3, B-2, C-1
(c) A-1, B-3, C-2 (d) A-2, B-1, C-3

8. The term "Googly" is associated with which of the following sports?

(a)

(b)

(c)

(d)

9. Saina Nehwal is associated with:
(a) Hockey (b) Basketball
(c) Badminton (d) Chess

10. Who is known as the Flying Sikh of India?
(a) Usain Bolt
(b) Milkha Singh
(c) Sachin Tendulkar
(d) Dhyan Chand

11. What kind of creature is Jerry who is always escaping from Tom?
(a) Cat (b) Wolf
(c) Mouse (d) Human

12. What is the name of blue bodied cat shown in image who is always pestered by three cockroaches?

(a) Jack (b) Jerry
(c) Oggy (d) Dee Dee

13. Which of the following statements is INCORRECT?
(a) Cristiano Ronaldo is a famous footballer.
(b) There are 11 players in each side in case of football.
(c) Dice is related to ludo.
(d) Carrom is an outdoor game.

14. Identify "X" and "Y".

Sachin Tendulkar	"X"
"Y"	Mary Kom

(a) X-Cricket, Y-Boxing
(b) X-Football, Y-Wrestling

(c) X-Hockey, Y-Badminton
(d) X- Cricket, Y-Tennis
15. Which of these is NOT associated with cricket?
(a) No ball
(b) Googly
(c) Leg Before Wicket
(d) Goal

ACHIEVERS SECTION

1. Who among the following played the role of PK in the movie PK?
   (a) Shah Rukh Khan
   (b) Salman Khan
   (c) Aamir Khan
   (d) Amitabh Bachchan

2. A famous robotic cat helps a boy named _____ in a famous cartoon series, Doraemon.
   (a) Shizuka   (b) Nobita
   (c) Suneo   (d) Gian

3. How many names of cartoon characters are hidden in the given word grid?

S	A	H	S	J	G	S	T
B	F	A	H	E	T	O	M
H	O	G	I	R	G	G	D
E	W	E	N	T	I	G	O

(a) 5   (b) 6
(c) 4   (d) 3

4. A checkered gameboard with 64 squares arranged in an _____ grid is called chess.
   (a) Eight-by-eight
   (b) Seven-by-seven
   (c) Six-by-six
   (d) Nine-by-nine

5. What is the highest number you can get by throwing a single dice?
   (a) 3   (b) 5
   (c) 6   (d) 1

Answer-Key

LEVEL 1

1. (c)	2. (a)	3. (c)	4. (a)	5. (b)
6. (b)	7. (a)	8. (a)	9. (a)	10. (a)
11. (b)	12. (a)	13. (a)	14. (b)	15. (c)
16. (c)	17. (b)	18. (a)	19. (c)	20. (a)
21. (b)	22. (a)	23. (b)	24. (a)	25. (d)

Sports and Entertainment

LEVEL 2

1. (d)	2. (b)	3. (c)	4. (d)	5. (b)
6. (a)	7. (a)	8. (a)	9. (c)	10. (b)
11. (c)	12. (c)	13. (d)	14. (a)	15. (d)

ACHIEVERS SECTION

| 1. (c) | 2. (b) | 3. (a) | 4. (a) | 5. (c) |

Answers with Explanations

LEVEL 1

2. Correct option is (a)
Explanation: The given picture shows a running goggle Swimming kit includes swimsuit, goggles, bathing caps, pull buoys, gloves, etc.

4. Correct option is (a)
Explanation: The given picture shows Salman Khan. He is a famous Indian actor who works in Hindi films.

5. Correct option is (b)
Explanation: Tom and Jerry is a famous cartoon show in which a mouse, Jerry, is always escaping from a cat, Tom.

6. Correct option is (b)
Explanation: Amitabh Bachchan is an Indian film actor and considered as one of the greatest actors in the history of Indian cinema.

9. Correct option is (a)
Explanation: In Kabaddi, there are two teams having seven players each who face off against each other.

10. Correct option is (a)
Explanation:

Cricket	11 players on each side
Basketball	5 players on each side
Baseball	9 players on each side
Chess	1 player on each side

11. Correct option is (b)
Explanation: A chessboard has 64 squares in eight-by-eight grid.

12. Correct option is (a)
Explanation: Hockey is being played in the given picture as it is played with the help of curved sticks and a ball.

13. Correct option is (a)
Explanation: Boxing gloves are

133

shown in the image. They are used far boxing.

15. **Correct option is (c)**
    Explanation: Cricket kit includes bat, ball, stumps, bails, leg guards, batting helmet, batting gloves, etc.

16. **Correct option is (c)**
    Explanation: Baseball, golf and rugby are outdoor games.

17. **Correct option is (b)**
    Explanation:

    | Novak Djokovic | Tennis |
    | Viswanathan Anand | Chess |
    | Mahesh Bhupathi | Tennis |
    | Milkha Singh | Runner |

19. **Correct option is (c)**
    Explanation: Ludo, Chess and carrom are indoor games.

20. **Correct option is (a)**
    Explanation: The sports person shown in the given picture is Serena William.

22. **Correct option is (a)**
    Explanation: Tennis is a sport in which players use racket to hit a ball over the net.

23. **Correct option is (b)**
    Explanation: Games which are played in open area are called outdoor games. For Example, baseball, hockey, cricket, soccer, etc.

24. **Correct option is (a)**
    Explanation: Games which are played under covered area are called indoor games. For example, ludo, chess, carrom, card games, etc.

25. **Correct option is (d)**
    Explanation: Badminton, volleyball, and tennis use net. In these sports, two teams are separated by a net.

LEVEL 2

1. **Correct option is (d)**
   Explanation: Cricket, snooker and hockey, all are played with a ball, whereas, badminton is played with a shuttlecock.

2. **Correct option is (b)**
   Explanation: The term LBW 6 (Leg Before Wicket) is used in cricket.

3. **Correct option is (c)**
   Explanation: Football, basketball and volleyball are played with the help of ball only, whereas, hockey is played with the help of a curved stick and a ball.

4. **Correct option is (d)**
   Explanation: Cricket, hockey and football, all are outdoor games, whereas snake & ladder is an indoor game.

5. **Correct option is (b)**
   Explanation: Football is played with a ball. Cricket is played with

Sports and Entertainment

a bat and a ball. Hockey is played with a curved stick and a ball. Polo is played with a flexible handle and a ball while riding on horseback.

6. **Correct option is (a)**
   Explanation: Sachin is known as 'Master Blaster' and 'God of Cricket' in India.

7. **Correct option is (a)**
   Explanation: Cricket is played with bat. Hockey is played with stick. Badminton is played with shuttlecock.

9. **Correct option is (c)**
   Explanation: Saina Nehwal is an Indian Badminton player. She is the first-ever badminton player from India who secured an Olympic medal.

10. **Correct option is (b)**
    Explanation: Milkha Singh is widely known as "The Flying Sikh". He defeated Abdul Khaliq in Pakistan in 1960 and got this nickname from General Ayub Khan of Pakistan.

11. **Correct option is (c)**
    Explanation: Tom & Jerry is a famous cartoon, in which Jerry, a is mouse, always escaping from tom, a cat.

12. **Correct option is (c)**
    Explanation: In the famous cartoon, Oggy & the Cockroaches, Oggy is a blue bodied cat who loves to eat and watch movies but is always pestered by three cockroaches.

13. **Correct option is (d)**
    Explanation: Carrom in an indoor game.

14. **Correct option is (a)**
    Explanation: Sachin Tendulkar is a cricket player while Mary Kom is a boxer.

15. **Correct option is (d)**
    Explanation: No ball, googly and leg before wicket(LBW) are associated with cricket, while goal is associated with football.

ACHIEVERS SECTION

1. **Correct option is (c)**
   Explanation: Aamir Khan played the lead role and name of his character was PK. PK (an alien) landed on the Earth and immediately loses his remote control.

2. **Correct option is (b)**
   Explanation: Doraemon is a famous Japanese cartoon in which a robotic cat called Doraemon always helps a boy Nobita.

3. **Correct option is (a)**
   Explanation: Bheem, Shinchan, Oggy, Tom, Patlu.

4. **Correct option is (a)**

   Explanation: Chess is played on a square board called chessboard with 64 squares arranged in an eight-by-eight grid.

5. **Correct option is (c)**

   Explanation: There are six face of a dice, having different number dots starting from 1 to 6 in which 6 is the highest number of dots.

How to make learning

Fun, Effective & Responsive

at the same time?

It's easy!
Scan the QR codes below

Famous Indian Sports Personalities · Games and Sports · Indoor and Outdoor Games

and get started!

Language and Literature

Group Words

Group	Common Combinations	
Bunch	flowers, roses, tulips, grapes, cherries, bananas, keys	
Crowd	people, admirers, protesters, kids, reporters, shoppers	
Flock	sheep, birds, geese, pigeons, gulls, gannets	
Gang	teenagers, youths, workers, youngers	

Compound Words

- Basket+Ball — Basketball
- Rain+Drop — Raindrop
- Cup+Cake — Cupcake
- Paint+Brush — Paintbrush
- Note+Book — Notebook

Sound Words

- Duck — Quack
- Clock — Tick Tock
- Bee — Buzz
- Drum — Bang
- Bell — Ring

Rhyming Words

- Pen Men
- Win Bin
- Sand Band
- Bag Rag
- Goat Boat

Homophones

- See Sea
- Dear Deer
- Son Sun
- Week Weak
- Hair Hare

Books & Their Authors

- Discovery Of India — Jawaharlal Nehru
- Gitanjali — Rabindra Nath Tagore
- Harry Potter — J.K.Rowling
- Making India Awesome — Chetan Bhagat
- My Country My Life — Lal Krishna Advani
- My Music My Life — Pandit Ravi Shankar
- My Unforgettable Memories — Mamta Banerjee
- Panchtantra — Vishnu Sharma
- Playing It My Way — Sachin Tendulkar
- Romeo and Juliet — William Shakespeare

137

CHAPTER 7
LANGUAGE AND LITERATURE

Learning Outcomes

Children would be able to:
- ✓ Know homophones, compound words, group words;
- ✓ Have rhyming fun;
- ✓ Understand different short stories;
- ✓ Recognise various famous books and their authors.

Concept Review

INTRODUCTION

Language is a body of words used to communicate with each other. Thus, it is important for everyone to share their thoughts and ideas. On the other hand, literature is nothing but books and writings published on a particular subject in a particular language and has lasting importance.

DID YOU KNOW?
A new word is added to the dictionary every two hours.

Rhyming Fun

★ **Ding, Dong, Bell**

Ding, dong, bell,
Pussy's in the well.
Who put her in?
Little Johnny Green.
Who pulled her out?
Little Tommy Stout.
What a naughty boy was that,

To try to drown poor pussy cat,
Who ne'er did him any harm,
But killed all the mice in the farmer's barn.

★ **Humpty Dumpty**

Humpty Dumpty sat on a wall,

Humpty Dumpty had a great fall;

All the king's horses and all the king's men

Couldn't put Humpty together again.

★ **Cobbler, Cobbler, Mend My Shoe**

Cobbler, cobbler, mend my shoe.
Get it done by half past two.
Half past two is much too late.
Get it done by half past eight.
Stitch it up and stitch it down.
And I'll give you half a crown.

★ **Baa, Baa, Black Sheep**

Baa, baa, black sheep,
Have you any wool?
Yes sir, yes sir,
Three bags full.
One for the master,
One for the dame,
And one for the little boy
Who lives down the lane.

★ **Hickory Dickory Dock**

Hickory, dickory, dock.

The mouse ran up the clock.

The clock struck one,

The mouse ran down,

Hickory, dickory, dock.

★ **Sound Words**

Duck	Quack
Clock	Tick Tock
Bee	Buzz
Drum	Bang
Bell	Ring
Pig	Oink
Cat	Meow
Thunder	Boom
Water	Splash

★ **Group Words**

- Group words are those which are used to refer to a collection of things as a whole.

Group	Common Combinations	Examples
Bunch	flowers, roses, tulips, grapes, cherries, bananas, keys	A bunch of keys.
Crowd	people, admirers, protesters, kids, reporters, shoppers	A crowd of people.
Flock	sheep, birds, geese, pigeons, gulls, gannets	A flock of birds.
Gang	teenagers, youths, workers, youngers	A gang of teenagers.
Herd	sheep, cattle, cows, goats, deer, elephants	A herd of cattle.
Pack	cards, dogs, hyenas, lies, wolves, hounds	A pack of cards.
Thunder	Boom	Boom of thunder
Water	Splash	Splash of the water

★ **Rhyming Words**

- Words which have similar sounds in the final stressed syllables and any following syllables of two or more words.

Pen	Men
Win	Bin
Sand	Band
Bag	Rag
Goat	Boat
Skip	Trip
Ring	Sing
Main	Pain

FUN TRIVIA

The longest word that is typed with only left hand on QWERTY keyboard is "Stewardesses".

Language and Literature

Meet	Greet
Book	Hook

★ **Homophones**

- Homophones are those words which have different but have the same sound.

1.	See	Sea
2.	Dear	Deer
3.	Son	Sun
4.	Week	Weak
5.	Hair	Hare
6.	Fair	Fare
7.	Idle	Idol
8.	No	Know
9.	Weight	Wait
10.	Prey	Pray
11.	Desert	Dessert
12.	Sale	Sail
13.	Night	Knight
14.	Break	Brake
15.	Bye	Buy

DID YOU KNOW?

There are "ghost words" that mean nothing. There are some words that appeared in the dictionary because of printing errors. The nonexistent word "dord" appeared in the dictionary for eight years in the mid-20th century. It later came to be known as "ghost word".

★ **Words that goes together**

- **Compound Words:** A compound word consists of two different words which together make a new meaning.

Basket+Ball	Basketball
Rain+Drop	Raindrop
Cup+Cake	Cupcake
Paint+Brush	Paintbrush
Note+Book	Notebook
Butter+Fly	Butterfly
Sun+Light	Sunlight
Good+Bye	Goodbye
Grand+Mother	Grandmother
Snow+Ball	Snowball
News+Paper	Newspaper

Story Time

- **Goldilocks**

There were three bears living in forest. There was a big bear, a middle bear, and a little wee bear. One day as they were leaving the house, a little girl named Goldilocks entered their home. The bears made porridge. Goldilocks tried the big bear's porridge but it was too hot; then she tried middle bear's porridge but it was too cold. Then she tried wee bear's porridge and it was good, so she ate it all. After that, she sat in all their seats. The big bear's seat was very heavy, the middle bear's seat was very soft, but the little bear's seat was right so she stayed there until the floor came out. Goldilocks felt tired so she went to the big bear's bed but it was too high on the head, the middle bear's bed was too high on the feet, but the wee bear's bed was just right so she slept there. The bears came home and noticed that someone had eaten their porridge, sat in all their seats, and laid in all their beds. The Goldilocks did not hear the voice of the big bear because it sounded like thunder, the voice of the middle bear sounded like a dream, but the sound of the wee bear woke Goldilocks and she saw three bears sitting on the edge of her bed. Goldilocks fled from the window. The bears never saw Goldilocks again.

- **Snow White**

A beautiful girl, Snow White, takes refuge in the woods in the house of seven dwarfs to hide from her stepmother, the wicked Queen. The Queen is jealous because she wants to be known as "the most beautiful woman in the world," and Snow White's beauty surpasses her own. But one day while the little ones (dwarfs) are in their diamond mine, the Queen arrives at their house disguised as an old woman selling apples and begs Snow White to bite the poisoned apple. The dwarfs, warned by the wild animals, rush home to chase the wicked queen, but it is too late to save Snow White from the poisonous apple. They put her in a glass box in the woods and mourned for her. She was saved by her good-looking prince charming by giving a first love kiss.

Language and Literature

★ Cinderella

Once upon a time, there was a lovely girl named Cinderella. She had a bad step-mother and two younger sisters. She worked hard all day. One day, they all went to the grand ball at the King's palace, leaving Cinderella behind. Cinderella was feeling sad and crying. Suddenly, a light flashed and the fairy godmother appeared.

In a flash, Cinderella turned into a beautiful princess with glass shoes. The fairy godmother found six mice playing near a pumpkin, in the kitchen. She turned mice into four shiny black horses and two coachmen and the pumpkin into a golden coach. The fairy godmother warned Cinderella to return before midnight. Cinderella went to the ball, the prince saw her and loved her.

They dance together all night long. When the clock struck twelve, Cinderella hurried to her cart leaving one of her slippers behind. The officer went to every house in town with a shoe until he found Cinderella. Prince and Cinderella lived happily ever after.

★ Sleeping Beauty

After the beautiful Princess Aurora is born into royalty, everyone gathers to celebrate. Everything is going well until the unwanted visitor, a bad legend. Maleficent curses the little princess and announces that she will die by pricking her finger on the spindle of a spinning wheel before sunset on her 16th birthday. Fortunately, one of the good fairies, Merryweather, changes this spell to give Aurora a great sleep, and the only way to wake her up is a true kiss from lover. When Aurora fell into a deep sleep after sticking her finger, everyone in the kingdom also fell asleep. The magic forest of thick thrones grew around the castle. One hundred years passed. The sleeping princess was just a story. One day, a prince came and found the princess asleep. She was so beautiful that he loved her. The prince kissed the princess.

It was a magical kiss. The princess woke up and saw the prince. She fell in love with the prince. When the princess woke up, everyone in the royal court woke up. The king and queen were very happy to see this beautiful prince. The prince and the princess got married and lived happily ever after.

★ **Famous Books and their Authors**

S. No.	Books	Authors
1.	Discovery of India	Jawaharlal Nehru
2.	Gitanjali	Rabindranath Tagore
3.	Harry Potter	J. K. Rowling
4.	Making India Awesome	Chetan Bhagat
5.	My Country My Life	Lal Krishna Advani

6.	My Music My Life	Pandit Ravi Shankar
7.	My Unforgettable Memories	Mamta Banerjee
8.	Panchtantra	Vishnu Sharma
9.	Playing It My Way	Sachin Tendulkar
10.	Romeo and Juliet	William Shakespeare

DID YOU KNOW?

The Panchatantra is a collection of folktales and fables that were believed to have been originally written in Sanskrit.

Multiple Choice Questions

LEVEL 1

1. Select the word that does not rhyme with other words.
   (a) Skip (b) Drip
   (c) Drop (d) Trip   **[2019]**

2. Chetan Bhagat is a famous _____.
   (a) singer (b) dancer
   (c) politician (d) writer   **[2017]**

3. Which one of the following is a story book?
   (a) Half Girlfriend
   (b) Romeo and Juliet
   (c) Panchatantra
   (d) None of these   **[2016]**

4. Match the following.

Column I		Column II
A.	Gitanjali	1. Shakespeare
B.	Harry Potter	2. Rabindranath Tagore
C.	Romeo and Juliet	3. J. K. Rowling

   (a) A-1, B-2, C-3 (b) A-3, B-2, C-1
   (c) A-2, B-1, C-3 (d) A-2, B-3, C-1
   [2015]

5. Jawaharlal Nehru wrote the book _____.
   (a) Discovery of India
   (b) India Discovery
   (c) Gitanjali
   (d) Harry Potter

6. The book written by Rabindranath Tagore is _____.
   (a) Discovery of India
   (b) Gitanjali
   (c) My Country My Life
   (d) My Unforgettable Memories

7. Which of these sounds does a clock make?
   (a) Slurp
   (b) Splash
   (c) Clap
   (d) Tick-Tock

8. Which of these goes with the word 'Paint'?
   (a) Key (b) Butter
   (c) Broom (d) Brush

9. A group of flowers is called _____.
   (a) Herd (b) Bunch
   (c) Pack (d) Gang

10. Choose the correct homonym pair.
    (a) Car-Care
    (b) Hair-Hare
    (c) Whole-Whose
    (d) Flour-For

11. Which of the following words goes with the word 'Sun'?
    (a) Moon (b) Ocean
    (c) Light (d) Key

12. Which word rhymes with the word 'Boat'?
    (a) Goat (b) Ship
    (c) Pen   (d) Yacht

13. Which word rhymes with word 'Book'?
    (a) Pen   (b) Pencil
    (c) Hook (d) Boat

14. Which of the following words goes with the word 'News'?
    (a) Book (b) Paper
    (c) Pen   (d) Sew

15. Which of the following words is the homophone of the word 'Deer'?
    (a) Dear (b) Bear
    (c) Hare (d) Tip

16. What is a 'group of keys' called?
    (a) Gang (b) Bunch
    (c) Shoal (d) School

17. Which of the following is not a pair of Homophones?
    (a) Break-Brake (b) Bye-Buy
    (c) Night-Knight (d) Pin-Win

18. The author of book 'Playing it My Way' is _____.
    (a) Sachin Tendulkar
    (b) Jawaharlal Nehru
    (c) Mamta Banerjee
    (d) Rabindranath Tagore

19. 'Making India Awesome' book is written by_____.
    (a) Sachin Tendulkar
    (b) Shakespeare
    (c) Chetan Bhagat
    (d) Rabindranath Tagore

20. Which word rhymes with 'crab'?
    (a) Map   (b) Grab
    (c) Jam   (d) Lamp

LEVEL 2

1. In a famous fairy tale, the Fairy Godmother turned _____ into a coach so that Cinderella could go to the Prince's Ball.
    (a) Mouse   (b) Potato
    (c) Pumpkin (d) Cockroach [2019]

2. Identify 'X' and 'Y'.

Lal Krishna Advani	'X'	Minister
'Y'	My Music My Live	Musician

   (a) X = Discovery of India; Y = Shakespeare
   (b) X = Shakespeare; Y = Discovery of India
   (c) X = My country My Life; Y = Pandit Ravi Shankar
   (d) None of these [2016]

3. Who had an encounter with the three bears?
    (a) Goldilocks
    (b) Snow White
    (c) Cinderella
    (d) Sleeping Beauty

4. In whose bed did Goldilocks fall fast asleep in the story Goldilocks and the three bears?
   (a) Father Bear
   (b) Mother Bear
   (c) Baby Bear
   (d) She Slept on the floor

5. For how long did Sleeping beauty sleep?
   (a) 50 years   (b) 100 years
   (c) 10 years   (d) 1000 years

   Direction: Read the following clues and complete the given word puzzle for questions 6-9.

   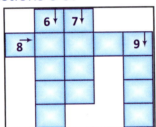

6. Rhyming word of 'Meet'.
   (a) Greet   (b) Meat
   (c) First   (d) Hall

7. The sound of thunder.
   (a) Bang   (b) Boom
   (c) Quack   (d) Ring

8. A group of youngers.
   (a) Bunch   (b) Crowd
   (c) Herd   (d) Cattle

9. The word which goes with rain.
   (a) Drop   (b) Sunny
   (c) Go Away   (d) Pain

   Direction: Read the following clues and complete the given word puzzle for questions 10-13.

   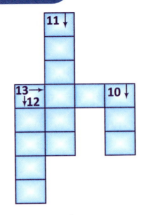

10. Rhyming word of 'Bag'.
    (a) Carry   (b) Rag
    (c) Rat   (d) Box

11. The sound of water.
    (a) Bang   (b) Splash
    (c) Buzz   (d) Quack

12. A group of pigeons.
    (a) Bunch   (b) Flock
    (c) Float   (d) Fair

13. The homophone of the word 'Fare'.
    (a) Fair   (b) Free
    (c) Flow   (d) Fast

14. Give a group name for the following set of words.
    sheep, cattle, cows, goats, deer, elephants
    (a) Cattle   (b) Herd
    (c) Gang   (d) Flock

15. **Statement A:** Harry Porter is written by Rowling.
    Statement B: She was a politician.
    (a) Statement A is correct
    (b) Statement B is correct
    (c) Both A and B are correct
    (d) None of these

Language and Literature

ACHIEVERS SECTION

Direction: Read the following rhyme and answer the questions from 1-5.

Baa, baa, black sheep,
Have you any wool?
Yes sir, yes sir,
Three bags full.
One for the master,
One for the dame,
And one for the little boy
Who lives down the lane.

1. What colour is the sheep?
   (a) White (b) Black
   (c) Yellow (b) Blue
2. How many bags of wool are there?
   (a) Two (b) Three
   (c) Four (d) Five
3. Where does the little boy live?
   (a) Town
   (b) City
   (c) Down the lane
   (d) Roof
4. Complete the sentence: Baa, Baa, Black Sheep, Have you any _____ .
   (a) Water (b) Wool
   (c) Cotton (d) Candy
5. Who is the wool for?
   (a) Master
   (b) Dame
   (c) Little boy
   (d) All of these

 Answer-Key

LEVEL 1

1. (c)	2. (d)	3. (c)	4. (d)	5. (a)
6. (b)	7. (d)	8. (d)	9. (b)	10. (b)
11. (c)	12. (a)	13. (c)	14. (b)	15. (a)
16. (b)	17. (d)	18. (a)	19. (c)	20. (b)

LEVEL 2

1. (c)	2. (c)	3. (a)	4. (c)	5. (b)
6. (a)	7. (b)	8. (b)	9. (a)	10. (b)
11. (b)	12. (b)	13. (a)	14. (b)	15. (a)

ACHIEVERS SECTION

| 1. (b) | 2. (b) | 3. (c) | 4. (b) | 5. (d) |

Answers with Explanations

LEVEL 1

1. **Correct option is (c)**
   Explanation: Skip, Drip, and Trip are rhyming words as they all end with an identical sound.

2. **Correct option is (d)**
   Explanation: Chetan Bhagat is a famous Indian writer. Some of his famous books are Half Girlfriend, 2 States, One Indian Girl, etc.

3. **Correct option is (c)**
   Explanation: The Panchatantra is a series of story books which includes various folktales and fables based on wisdom, courage, bravery, wickedness, cruelty and so on.

5. **Correct option is (a)**
   Explanation: During imprisonment for participating in Quit India Movement, Pt. Jawaharlal Nehru wrote the book 'The Discovery of India', based on Indian History.

6. **Correct option is (b)**
   Explanation: Gitanjali was written by Rabindranath Tagore, which is a collection of poems.

8. **Correct option is (d)**
   Explanation:
   Paint+Brush = Paintbrush
   Paintbrush is a brush which is used to apply paint on a picture or surface.

10. **Correct option is (b)**
    Explanation: The words, 'Hair' and 'Hare' have same pronunciation.

11. **Correct option is (c)**
    Explanation: Sun+Light=Sunlight
    Sunlight is the light which we get from sun during the day.

12. **Correct option is (a)**
    Explanation: The words, 'boat' and 'goat' end with an identical sound.

13. **Correct option is (c)**
    Explanation: The words, 'Book' and 'Hook' end with an identical sound.

14. **Correct option is (b)**
    Explanation:
    News + Paper = Newspaper
    A paper containing news, article, advertisements, etc.

15. **Correct option is (a)**
    Explanation: The words, 'Deer' and 'Dear' have same pronunciation.

16. Correct option is (b)

Explanation: A bunch is a group of things which are of same kind, for example, flowers, keys, etc.

17. Correct option is (d)

Explanation: 'Pin' and 'Win' are rhyming words as they are ending with an identical sound.

18. Correct option is (a)

Explanation: Sachin Tendulkar is a former Indian cricketer and 'Playing It My Way' is an autobiography of him.

19. Correct option is (c)

Explanation: 'Making India Awesome' is a book written by an Indian writer, Chetan Bhagat. This book is about how we, youth, can make India awesome.

20. Correct option is (b)

Explanation: 'Crab' and 'Grab' are rhyming words as they are ending with an identical sound.

LEVEL 2

1. Correct option is (c)

Explanation: In a famous fairy tale, Cinderella, the Fairy Godmother turned pumpkin into a coach, four mice into four horses and two mice into two coachmen so that Cinderella could go to the Prince's ball.

3. Correct option is (a)

Explanation: Goldilocks had an encounter with three bears when she was sleeping on the bed of the little bear. The sound of the wee bear woke Goldilocks and she saw three bears sitting on the edge of her bed.

4. Correct option is (c)

Explanation: Goldilocks fell asleep in little bear's bed as father bear's bed was too high on the head, mother bear's bed was too high on the feet, but the little bear's bed was just right for her.

5. Correct option is (b)

Explanation: Sleeping Beauty which was Princess Aurora, fell into a deep sleep after sticking her finger in a spinning wheel. She woke up after 100 years by a true lover's kiss.

6. Correct option is (a)

Explanation: 'Meet' and 'Meat' have same pronunciation.

9. Correct option is (a)

Explanation: Rain+Drop
    A drop of rain.

10. Correct option is (b)

Explanation: 'Bag' and 'Rag' are rhyming words as they are ending with an identical sound.

12. Correct option is (b)

Explanation: Flock is a group of birds (or pigeons) assembled together.

13. **Correct option is (a)**

    Explanation: The words, 'Fare' and 'Fair' have same pronunciation.

15. **Correct option is (a)**

    Explanation: J. K. Rowling is a famous British author, who wrote a book, 'Harry Porter'.

ACHIEVERS SECTION

1. **Correct option is (b)**

    Explanation: The colour of sheep is black. It is mentioned in the first line of the poem.

2. **Correct option is (b)**

    Explanation: There are three bags of wool. It is mentioned in the fourth line of the poem.

3. **Correct option is (c)**

    Explanation: The little boy lives down the lane. It is mentioned in the last line of the poem.

4. **Correct option is (b)**

    Explanation: 'Baa, Baa, Black Sheep, Have you any wool'
    These are the first two lines of the poem.

5. **Correct option is (d)**

    Explanation: There are three bags of wool. One for the master, one for the dame, and one for the little boy.

How to make learning
Fun, Effective & Responsive
at the same time?

It's easy!
Scan the QR codes below

Collective Noun

Rhyming Words

and get started!

Numbers' Magic

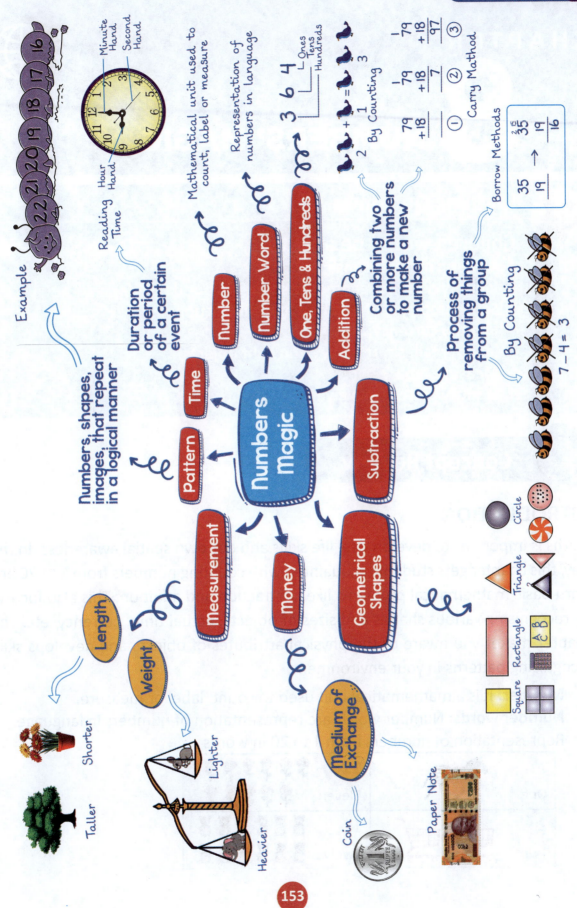

CHAPTER 8
NUMBERS' MAGIC

Learning Outcomes

Children would be able to
- ✓ Develop number sense;
- ✓ Identify different geometric shapes in our daily life;
- ✓ Solve problems of addition and subtraction;
- ✓ Identify currency;
- ✓ Identify tall, short, heavy and light objects;
- ✓ Measure time;
- ✓ Identify pattern in a given series.

Concept Review

INTRODUCTION

Maths is important to develop vital life skills and our own spatial awareness. In this way, this chapter gets students acquainted with counting numbers from 1 to 20 and learn basic mathematical problems like subtraction and addition. This also focuses on recognising various shapes and sizes of objects, actual time, currency, etc. This chapter makes you aware of the physical attributes of objects and develops skills recognising patterns in your environment.

- **Number:** It is a mathematical unit used to count, label or measure.
- **Number words:** Number words are representation of numbers in language.
- Representation of numbers from 1 to 20 in words

| 1 One | 🦓 | 11 Eleven | 🌼🌼🌼🌼🌼🌼🌼🌼🌼🌼 |
| 2 Two | 🛒🛒 | 12 Twelve | 🧸🧸🧸🧸🧸🧸🧸🧸🧸🧸🧸🧸 |

Numbers' Magic

3 Three		13 Thirteen	
4 Four		14 Fourteen	
5 Five		15 Fifteen	
6 Six		16 Sixteen	
7 Seven		17 Seventeen	
8 Eight		18 Eighteen	
9 Nine		19 Nineteen	
10 Ten		20 Twenty	

> **AMAZING FACTS**
> 'Four' is the only number in the English language that is spelt with the same number of letters as the number itself.

> **AMAZING FACTS**
> The word "hundred" comes from the old Norse term, "hundrath", which actually means 120 and not 100.

★ **Concept of Ones, Tens, and Hundreds**
These are places of digits in a number.

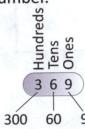

- **Addition:** It is the process of calculating total or sum of two or more values, digits or numbers.
- To find the total number of one-digit numbers:
  ▪ Count the first number on your fingers.
  ▪ Count the second number on your fingers.
  ▪ The total number of fingers is the result.

For example:

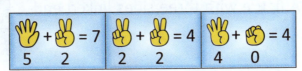

- Carry method of doing Addition

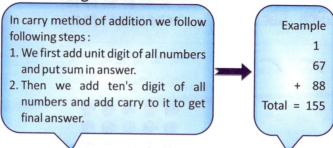

★ **Subtraction:**

It is the process of calculating how many are left or how many more or less.

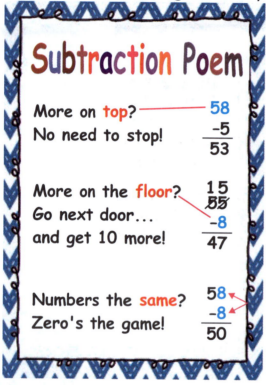

★ **Geometrical Shapes:**

A geometric shape is a figure closed by combining points, lines or curves. There are four basic geometric shapes which are:
- **Circle:** A perfect round shape.
- **Square:** A figure with four equal sides.
- **Rectangle:** A figure with four sides, in which opposite sides are parallel and equal.
- **Triangle:** A figure with three sides linked end-to-end.

Triangle

Circle

Rectangle

Square

Numbers' Magic

★ **Money:**
Money is a medium of exchange, i.e., buying and selling of objects.
- Coins currently used in India:

- Paper Notes used in India:

DID YOU KNOW?
Indian Rupees is not made of paper as it appears to be, it is rather made of Cotton and Rag. It is the pulp of cotton, balsam, dyes, and textile fibers.

Rupees Two Thousand

Rupees Fifty

Rupees Five Hundred

Rupees Twenty

Rupees Two Hundred

Rupees Ten

Rupees One Hundred

★ **Weight:**
Weight is a quantity or amount of mass in an object.
- **Heavy Objects:** Things which have more weight are called heavy. Usually heavy things are large in size and hard. For example, truck, car, scooter, bed, almirah, etc.

- **Light Objects:** Things which have less weight are called light. Light things are easy to carry. For example, feather, leaf, paper, pencil, etc.

- **Comparing Heavy and Light**

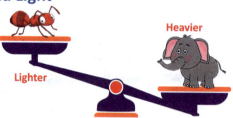

★ **Length:**
Length is a measurement which tells how long an object is.
- **Long or Tall Object:** An object which has more height or length is called a tall or long object. For example, train, tree, bamboo, etc.

- **Short Object:** An object which has less height or length is called a short object. For example, eraser, bowl, etc.

- **Comparing Tall and Short**

★ **Time**
- Measuring units of time are seconds, minutes and hours. For example, 3 hours; 20 minutes; 40 seconds.

Numbers' Magic

- When we measure time, we measure the duration or period of a certain event. For example, Meera studied for 3 hours 45 minutes.
- Now just remember:
    - 24 hours = 1 day
    - 1 hour = 60 minutes
    - 1 minute = 60 seconds
- **Clock Indicating Time**

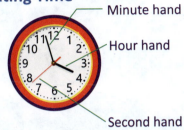

DID YOU KNOW?

There are 86,400 seconds in a day.

- The hour hand moves from one number to the next in 1 hour.
- The hour hand takes two complete round in a day.
- The minute hand takes 1 hour to complete one round.

★ **Reading Time from a Clock**
- When a minute hand is at 12, then the actual time is the number that is indicated by the hour hand. For example, the given clock indicates that the time is 9 O' Clock as minute hand is at 12 and hour hand is at 9.

- If hour hand is somewhere between 2 numbers, for example, between 9 and 10, minute hand is at a particular number, for example, at 5, and the time is 9:25 and it will be read as 25 minutes past 9.

★ **Calendar:**
It is a systematic arrangement of days, weeks, months and year to show various periods of time.

Calendar 2021

- **Days in a Week:** A week consists of seven days which are as follows:

Days of the Week

- Monday
- Tuesday
- Wednesday
- Thursday
- Friday
- Saturday
- Sunday

- **Months in a Year:** There are 12 months in a year, which are:

Months in a Year

1. January
2. February
3. March
4. April
5. May
6. June
7. July
8. August
9. September
10. October
11. November
12. December

Numbers' Magic

- **Patterns:** This is all about—numbers, shapes, images—that repeat in a logical manner. One needs to make logical connections in the given pattern to understand what comes next.

Multiple Choice Questions

LEVEL 1

1. There are three kittens. How many ears are there?
   (a) 3 (b) 4
   (c) 6 (d) 8 **[2015]**

2. How many 🐟 are there in the box?
   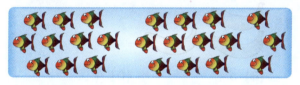
   (a) 22 (b) 23
   (c) 19 (d) 21 **[2015]**

3. I have 6 .
   I have given 4 more.
   How many do I have?
   (a) 12 (b) 2
   (c) 10 (d) 24

4. Which clock shows 5 O' clock?
   (a)  (b)
   (c)  (d)

5. Which bunch shows two more bananas than given bananas?
   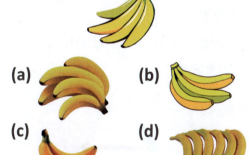

6. There are 7 ones and 4 tens.
   (a) 47 (b) 74
   (c) 64 (d) 46

7. _____ comes after May but before July.
   (a) April
   (b) June
   (c) August
   (d) December

8. Which of the following is lightest?

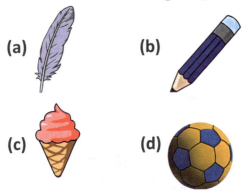

9. Which of the following numbers has 5 tens?
   (a) 54   (b) 46
   (c) 45   (d) 68

10. Look at the shape shown in the picture. What is it called?
    (a) Triangle
    (b) Circle
    (c) Square
    (d) Rectangle

11. How many matchsticks form a triangle?

    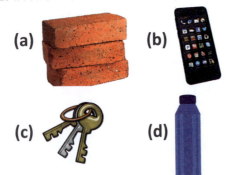

    (a) 4   (b) 3
    (c) 2   (d) 6

12. Which item is the heaviest?

13. Which shape has the smallest number of sides?

    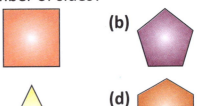

14. _____ mangoes are outside the box and _____ apples are inside the box.

    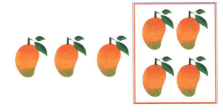

    (a) 2, 3   (b) 4, 5
    (c) 3, 4   (d) 1, 3

15.

    (a) 3   (b) 4
    (c) 2   (d) 1

16. Raja had four apples. He ate one of them. How many apples are left?

    (a) 2   (b) 3
    (c) 1   (d) 4

17. What are the missing numbers on the number line?

    (a) 5, 7   (b) 8, 7
    (c) 5, 6   (d) 4, 7

18. 4 + 0 = ?
    (a) 4   (b) 1
    (c) 2   (d) 3

19. 6 − 0 = ?
    (a) 4   (b) 5
    (c) 6   (d) 7

20. Find the odd one out.
    (a) May   (b) September
    (c) Sunday   (d) August

21. Identify the group with more objects.

    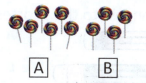

    (a) A   (b) B
    (c) Equal in both (a) and (b)
    (d) Neither (a) nor (b)

22. 21 + 19 = ?
    (a) 30   (b) 40
    (c) 31   (d) 39

23. 8 + ___ = 13
    (a) 6   (b) 7
    (c) 5   (d) 9

24. _____ is the sixth day of week.
    (a) Tuesday
    (b) Monday
    (c) Saturday
    (d) Friday

25. _____ comes between October and December.
    (a) January
    (b) February
    (c) September
    (d) November

LEVEL 2

1. How many more teddies should be crossed (x) to show 5 uncrossed teddies?

   (a) 5   (b) 2
   (c) 3   (d) 8   **[2019]**

2. Find the missing number in the given number pattern.

   (a) 15
   (b) 16
   (c) 21
   (d) 18   **[2019]**

3. Find the missing figure in the given figure pattern.

(a) (b) 🟪
(c) 🟠 (d) 🟨 **[2018]**

4. Which statement will make this equation complete?

   30____ 15 _____ 27

   (a) < and >   (b) < and <
   (c) > and >   (d) > and <

   [2017]

5. Complete the number pattern given below:

   The missing number is _____
   (a) 23   (b) 27
   (c) 24   (d) 20   **[2016]**

6. Mukul, Raghav, and Aryan are eating fruits on a hot summer day. Mukul and Raghav do not like grapes. Who likes to eat grapes?
   (a) Mukul
   (b) Raghav
   (c) Aryan
   (d) None of these   **[2016]**

7. _____ is fifth from right hand.

(a) (b)

(c) (d)

8. A rectangle has _____ curved line(s).
   (a) 0   (b) 1
   (c) 2   (d) 4

9. Arrange the following pencils from the longest to the shortest.

   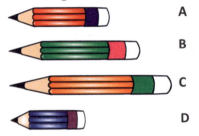

   (a) A, B, C, D   (b) D, C, B, A
   (c) C, B, A, D   (d) C, A, B, D

10. What is the descending order of 67, 87, 77, 57?
    (a) 87, 77, 67, 57
    (b) 57, 67, 77, 87
    (c) 57, 77, 67, 87
    (d) 87, 77, 57, 67

11. Which of the following is heavier than  ?

(c)  (d)

12. Which of the following is lighter than ?

   (a)  (b)

   (c)   (d)

13. There is/are _____ more circle(s) than triangles in the given figure.

    (a) 7   (b) 8
    (c) 9   (d) 1

14. This figure is made up of _____ triangles.

    (a) 3   (b) 2
    (c) 4   (d) 6

15. Select the incorrect match.

	Column I	Column II
A.	Circle	⭕
B.	Triangle	🍕
C.	Square	
D.	Rectangle	

16. What is the missing number in the given pattern?

    △3 △2 △5   △2 △5 △7
    △4 △? △6

    (a) 2   (b) 5
    (c) 4   (d) 3

17. How many Rs. 30?
    (a) 1   (b) 2
    (c) 3   (d) 4

18. There are _____ groups of 3 pens.

    (a) 5   (b) 3
    (c) 4   (d) 6

19. Who among the following is holding maximum number?

    (a)  2 tens 2 ones   (b)  3 tens 3 ones

    (c)  3 tens 2 ones   (d) 2 tens 1 ones

20. What comes in between?

(a) 24   (b) 42
(c) 36   (d) 32

ACHIEVERS SECTION

1. Rohit has a note of 100. He want to buy two items. Which of the following two item can he buy?

   (a) Gift box and Cap
   (b) Dress and Cap
   (c) Dress and Toy bike
   (d) Toy bike and Gift box   [2019]

2. Study the given picture carefully and fill in the blanks.

   Esha Aman Ali Nidhi Ritik
   Ali is taller than ___P___ but shorter than Ritik, ___Q___ is the shortest and ___R___ is the tallest.

	P	Q	R
A.	Nidhi	Aman	Ritik
B.	Aman	Aman	Nidhi
C.	Nidhi	Aman	Esha
D.	Aman	Nidhi	Ritik

   [2018]

3. Which of the following options shows the correct amount of money as the cost of the given toy car?

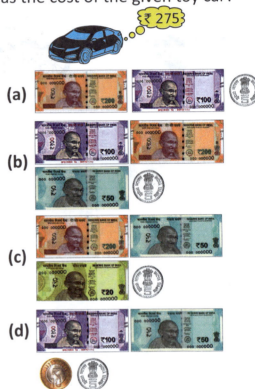

   [2018]

Directions (Qs. 4 & 5): Three children have different three birth months, but were all born in the same year. Mayank was born in April. Anshul was born after Mayank but before Shubham.

4. Who is the youngest?
   (a) Mayank
   (b) Anshul
   (c) Shubham
   (d) None of these   [2017]

5. Who is the oldest ?
   (a) Anshul
   (b) Mayank
   (c) Shubham
   (d) None of these   **[2017]**

Answer-Key

LEVEL 1

1. (c)	2. (b)	3. (c)	4. (a)	5. (d)
6. (a)	7. (b)	8. (a)	9. (a)	10. (c)
11. (b)	12. (a)	13. (c)	14. (c)	15. (a)
16. (b)	17. (a)	18. (a)	19. (c)	20. (c)
21. (a)	22. (b)	23. (c)	24. (c)	25. (d)

LEVEL 2

1. (b)	2. (b)	3. (b)	4. (d)	5. (b)
6. (c)	7. (c)	8. (a)	9. (c)	10. (a)
11. (d)	12. (c)	13. (a)	14. (a)	15. (c)
16. (a)	17. (c)	18. (b)	19. (b)	20. (c)

ACHIEVERS SECTION

| 1. (b) | 2. (c) | 3. (c) | 4. (c) | 5. (b) |

Answers with Explanations

LEVEL 1

1. **Correct option is (c)**
   Explanation: A kitten has 2 ears. Thus, 2+2+2 =6.

2. **Correct option is (b)**
   Explanation: 10 in first group, 10 in second group, and 3 in third group 10+10+3=23

3. **Correct option is (c)**
   Explanation: 6+4=10
   IIIIII + IIII = IIIIIIIIII

4. **Correct option is (a)**
   Explanation: Hour hand is at 5 and minute hand is at 12

5. **Correct option is (d)**

   Explanation: Given bunch has 4 bananas. To show 2 more bananas, a bunch should have 6 bananas.

   4+2=6

   IIII + II = IIIIII

6. **Correct option is (a)**

   Explanation:

   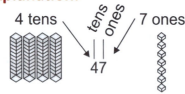

7. **Correct option is (b)**

   Explanation: 5th Month of a year – May

   6th Month of a year – June

   7th Month of a year – July

9. **Correct option is (a)**

   Explanation:

   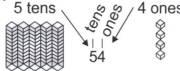

10. **Correct option is (c)**

    Explanation: Square is a figure with four equal sides.

11. **Correct option is (b)**

    Explanation: A triangle has 3 edges, thus 3 matchsticks are required.

12. **Correct option is (a)**

    Explanation: Bricks are the hardest item among all.

13. **Correct option is (c)**

    Explanation: Except triangle which has 3 sides, all other shapes has four or more than four sides.

15. **Correct option is (a)**

    Explanation: 2+1=3

    II + I = III

18. **Correct option is (a)**

    Explanation:

    $$4 + 0 = 4$$

20. **Correct option is (c)**

    Explanation: Sunday is a day in a week. May, August and September are months in a year.

21. **Correct option is (a)**

    Explanation: Number of Objects in Group A = 6

    Number of Objects in Group B = 4

22. **Correct option is (b)**

    Explanation:

    ```
      1
      2 1
    + 1 9
    -----
      4 0
    ```

23. **Correct option is (c)**

    Explanation: 8+5=13

    IIIIIIII+IIIII=IIIIIIIIIIIII

24. **Correct option is (c)**

    Explanation: 1st – Monday, 2nd – Tuesday, 3rd – Wednesday, 4th – Thursday, 5th – Friday, 6th – Saturday

25. **Correct option is (d)**

    Explanation: October – November – December.

LEVEL 2

1. **Correct option is (b)**
   Explanation: Total no. of teddies is 10. To show 5 uncrossed teddies, there should be 5 crossed teddies. 3 are already crossed. 2 more needs to be crossed as 2 + 3 = 5.

2. **Correct option is (b)**
   Explanation:
   4 + 4 = 8
   8 + 4 = 12
   12 + 4 = 16
   16 + 4 = 20

3. **Correct option is (b)**
   Explanation: Pattern: Triangle – Square – Circle – Rectangle

5. **Correct option is (b)**
   Explanation:
   7+3=10
   10+7=17
   17+3=20
   20+7=27
   27+3=30

7. **Correct option is (c)**
   Explanation:

   7   6   5   4   3   2   1

10. **Correct option is (a)**
    Explanation: Descending order is the arrangement of numbers from largest to smallest.

11. **Correct option is (d)**
    Explanation: A bed is larger in size than a chair.

12. **Correct option is (c)**
    Explanation: Eraser is smaller in size than a ball.

13. **Correct option is (a)**
    Explanation: Total number of circles=13
    Total number of triangles= 6
    13 – 6 = 7

15. **Correct option is (c)**
    Explanation: The shape given in column b is rectangular.

16. **Correct option is (a)**
    Explanation:
    3 + 2 = 5
    2 + 5 = 7
    4 + 2 = 6

17. **Correct option is (c)**
    Explanation: 1 coin = Rs.10
    Rs. 10+ Rs. 10+ Rs. 10= Rs. 30

18. **Correct option is (b)**
    Explanation: Total number of pens is 15.
    5+5+5=15

19. **Correct option is (b)**
    Explanation: 2 tens, 2 ones=22
    3 tens, 3 ones=33
    3 tens, 2 ones=32
    2 tens, 1 ones=21
    33>32>22>21

20. **Correct option is (c)**
    Explanation: 9 + 9 = 18
    18 + 9 = 27
    27 + 9 = 36
    36 + 9 = 45

ACHIEVERS SECTION

1. **Correct option is (b)**
   Explanation: 50 + 45 = 95 and 95 < 100, thus, he can buy a dress and a cap from Rs. 100.

3. **Correct option is (c)**
   Explanation: (a) 200+100+5=305
   (b) 100 + 100 + 50 + 5 = 255
   (c) 200 + 50 + 20 + 5 = 275
   (d) 100 + 50 + 10 + 5 = 165

4. **Correct option is (c)**
   Explanation: Correct order of birth: Mayank - Anshul - Shubham

5. **Correct option is (b)**
   Explanation: Correct order of birth: Mayank - Anshul - Shubham

How to make learning
Fun, Effective & Responsive
at the same time?

It's easy!
Scan the QR codes below

Geometrical Shapes   Number in Figures and Words

and get started!

Life Skills

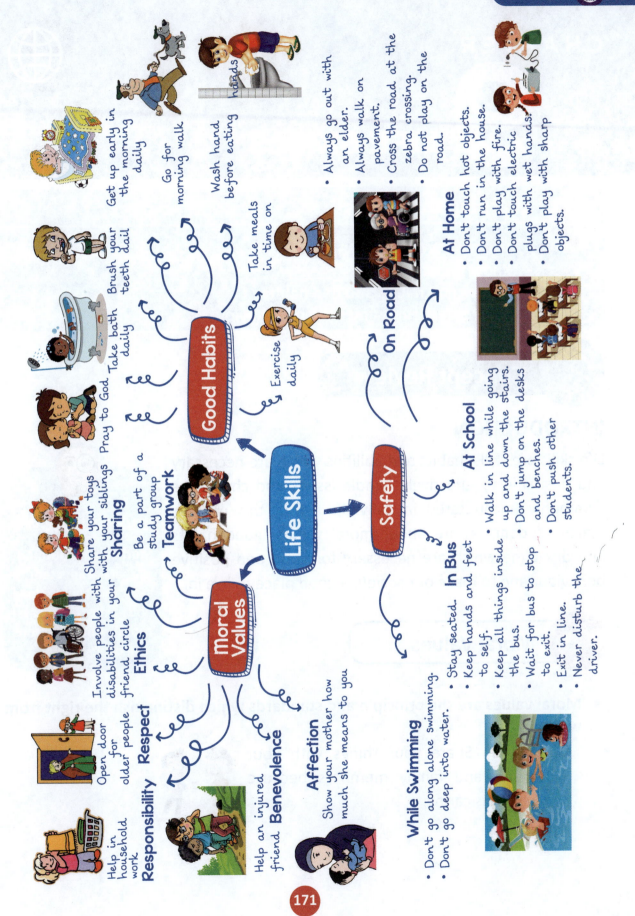

CHAPTER 9
LIFE SKILLS

Learning Outcomes

Children would be able to:
- Know moral values;
- Know good habits and bad habits;
- Obey safety rules and code of behaviour.

Concept Review

INTRODUCTION

Life skills are skills, habits and abilities which are necessary and desirable to effectively handle issues and challenges commonly encountered in daily life. Thus, this chapter makes students aware about moral values, good habits and discipline which are necessary for good and positive behaviour and to make our society a good place to live in.

DID YOU KNOW?

Students in South Korea are expected to stay and help clean and tidy the classroom when lessons are over.

Moral Values

★ Moral values are the principle and standards which distinguish the right from wrong.

1. **Sharing:** Share your things with your friends and family members because sharing is caring.

172

Life Skills

2. **Respect:** Respect everyone regardless of their age or social status.

3. **Teamwork:** Divide whole work into small tasks and then do your share to complete that work effectively and on time.

4. **Responsibility:** Be a dependable and reliable person, that is, committed to complete their obligations.

5. **Benevolence:** Be kind to people and help others.

6. **Ethics:** Recognize what is wrong and what is right, what is good and what is evil, what is appropriate and what is inappropriate and do right things.

7. **Affection:** Show your love and affection for the people in your life.

★ **Good habits**

Habits are our routine behaviour which we follow repeatedly and we even don't get to know when we acquire them.

Good habits lead to good manners which enable to be friend with good people. Good people means good environment. This ultimately leads to happy and peaceful life.

AMAZING FACTS

If you don't floss, you miss cleaning 40% of your tooth surfaces. Make sure you brush and floss twice a day!

★ **Do's**
- Brush your teeth twice a day.
- Always wash your hands before and after eating.
- Take shower daily and keep yourself clean.
- Comb your hair daily.
- Wake up early and sleep on time.
- Always use golden words while talking to others, which are 'Thank You'.
- 'Please', 'Welcome' and 'Sorry'.
- Pray to god daily.
- Go for morning walk daily.
- Keep your surroundings clean and don't litter public places.
- Eat healthy food.

★ **Don'ts**
- Don't litter in open area or streets.
- Don't quarrel with others.
- Don't bite your nails.
- Don't watch TV too much.
- Don't lie down while reading.
- Don't put anything in your ears.
- Don't put finger in your mouth and nose.

★ **Table Manners**
- Come to the table with clean hands and face.
- Put your napkin on your lap.
- Stay seated and sit upright.
- Keep elbows off the table while eating.
- Chew with your mouth closed and don't talk until you've swallowed.
- Say "Please pass the…" instead of reaching.
- Don't make rude noises like burping or slurping.

Life Skills

- Ask to be excused when finished.
- Thank your host or whoever prepared the meal.

★ **Safety Rules**

Accidents can occur anywhere, so to avoid accidents, we should take care of safety rules at home, at school and on road.

Safety at Home:
- Don't touch hot objects.
- Don't run in the house.
- Don't play with fire.
- Don't touch electric plugs with wet hands.
- Don't play with sharp objects.
- Don't open the door for strangers.
- Don't throw fruit peels on floor.
- Don't take medicine on your own.

Safety on Road
- Always go out with an elder.
- Always walk on pavement.
- Cross the road at the zebra crossing.
- Do not play on the road.
- Before crossing the road, look to the right and to the left. Cross the road only when it is clear.

DID YOU KNOW?

Traffic lights control traffic. There are three lights which are:
1. Red: Driver should stop his vehicle.
2. Green: Driver should start driving or keep driving.
3. Yellow: Driver should slow down his vehicle as light is about to turn red.

Safety at School
- Walk in line while going up and down the stairs.
- Don't jump on the desks and benches.
- Don't push other students.

Safety in Bus
- Stay seated.
- Keep hands and feet to self.
- Keep all things inside the bus.
- Wait for the bus to stop to exit.
- Exit in line.
- Never disturb the driver.

Safety while Swimming
- Don't go alone for swimming.
- Don't go deep into water.

175

Multiple Choice Questions

LEVEL 1

1. While eating in a restaurant, where should you place your napkin?
   (a) On the table
   (b) On your lap
   (c) Under your plate
   (d) On the back of your chair [2019]

2. Which of the following activity is not safe?
   (a)
   (b)
   (c)
   (d) Both (a) and (b) [2019]

3. Before going to bed, you should :
   (a) Read a book
   (b) Pack your school bag for the next day
   (c) Brush your teeth
   (d) All of these [2019]

4. Select the action which is safe.
   (a) (b)
   (c)  (d)
   [2018]

5. Comb your hair _____.
   (a) daily
   (b) twice a day
   (c) once in a week
   (d) All of the above

6. While walking on the road always walk _____ .
   (a) on the pavement
   (b) on the road
   (c) on the divider
   (d) while moving the bus

7. Which kind of habit is this?

   Wake up early in the morning .
   (a) Good   (b) Bad
   (c) Unsafe   (d) Untidy

8. Footpath should be used for _____.
   (a) Playing
   (b) Walking
   (c) Dancing
   (d) Both (b) and (c)

9. What is the first thing we should do after getting up in the morning?

   (a)   (b)

   (c)   (d)

10. Which of the following picture represents a bad habit?

    (a)    (b)

    (c)   (d)

11. Don't go deep into the water while _____ .

    (a) walking
    (b) sleeping
    (c) swimming
    (d) skiing

12. Match the following.

Column I		Column II
A.	Don't play with fire	1.
B.	Don't run on the road	2.
C.	Don't play with sharp objects	3.
D.	Don't touch electric fitting	4.

(a) A-4, B-3, C-2, D-1
(b) A-3, B-4, C-2, D-1
(c) A-2, B-3, C-4, D-1
(d) A-4, B-1, C-2, D-3

13. Wash your _____ before each meal.

    (a) stomach
    (b) knees
    (c) hands
    (d) elbow

14. Which of the following is a bad habit?

    (a)

    (b)

    (c)

    (d) All of the above

15. We should _____ twice a day.
    (a) Brush our teeth
    (b) Wash clothes
    (c) Trim nails
    (d) Throw rubbish on road
16. Identify which of the following is incorrect?
    (a) Wash your hands before eating.
    (b) Eat healthy food.
    (c) Go deep into water while swimming.
    (d) Inform your teacher when you get hurt.
17. Which of these is not a correct table manner?
    (a) Eat the food quietly.
    (b) Say 'excuse me' before leaving the dinner table.
    (c) Chew with your mouth closed while eating.
    (d) Rest elbows on the table while eating.
18. Which kind of habit is this?

    (a) Good   (b) Bad
    (c) Unsafe   (d) Untidy
19. Which kind of habit is this?

    (a) Good   (b) Bad
    (c) Unsafe   (d) Untidy
20. Before going to school, you should:
    (a) Brush your teeth
    (b) Take breakfast
    (c) Have lunch
    (d) Both (a) and (b)
21. Sleeping very little is a _____ habit.
    (a) Good   (b) Bad
    (c) Unsafe   (d) Untidy
22. Sam likes to _____ his face every morning.

    (a) wash
    (b) wipe
    (c) brush
    (d) None of these
23. Fill in the gap :

    _LE_P W_L_
    (a) SE EL   (b) SE LE
    (c) SE AL   (d) EO EL
24. Suhan likes to _____.

    (a) drink water
    (b) sleep well
    (c) wash face
    (d) eat well

25. Match the following.

Column I Habits		Column II Related Pictures	
A.	Eating a lot of junk food	1.	
B.	Getting enough sleep	2.	
C.	Biting nails	3.	
D.	Hand Hygiene	4.	

(a) A-3, B-4, C-2, D-1
(b) A-4, B-3, C-2, D-1
(c) A-2, B-4, C-1, D-3
(d) A-3, B-4, C-1, D-2

LEVEL 2

1. Which of the following is the correct thing to do, if there is too much dust in the air you breathe?
   (a) Eat fried food
   (b) Run fast
   (c) Cover your nose with a handkerchief
   (d) Drink less water **[2019]**

2. Which of the following is incorrect regarding the safety rules in the playground?
   (a) Never climb up the front of slides.
   (b) Walk in front of swings if someone is swinging.
   (c) Avoid using broken equipment.
   (d) Sit facing each other on the seesaw. **[2019]**

3. If you get proper sleep at night then, _____.
   (a) You will feel sleepy the whole next day.
   (b) You will be fresh and full of energy the next day.
   (c) You will find it difficult to get up on time next morning.
   (d) You will not be attentive in the class next day. **[2018]**

4. Select the correct match.

(a)	When you make a mistake, say	Hello
(b)	When someone helps you, say	Thank you
(c)	When you pick up the phone, say	Good bye
(d)	Before you finish a call on the phone, say	I am sorry

[2018]

5. If your friend asks for your toys, you should_____.
   (a) Totally ignore him
   (b) Share the toys with him
   (c) Complain to your parents
   (d) Fight with him **[2018]**

6. Which of the following is not a healthy habit?
   (a) Samira plays on the stairs.
   (b) Ravi wakes up early in the morning.
   (c) Radha eats healthy food.
   (d) Sudhir takes bath daily.

7. If your classmate stole something, you should:
   (a) tell the teacher
   (b) help him in stealing
   (c) ignore him
   (d) keep it a secret

8. State whether the following statements are true or false.
   (a) We should push others to go ahead.
   (b) We should not throw rubbish on road.
   (c) We should stay late and watch TV.
   (a) F, T, F   (b) T, T, T
   (c) F, F, T   (d) T, T, F

9. What is the first thing you do when guests come to your home?
   (a) Greet them with a smile
   (b) Say Goodbye to them
   (c) Push them
   (d) Ignore them

10. When your friend gives you a gift, you should say _____.
    (a) Thank You   (b) Sorry
    (c) Welcome   (d) Please

11. Playing with _____ can cause a fire.
    (a) Match stick (b) Knife
    (c) Needle   (d) Paper

12. Consider the following statements:
    Statement A : We should not play with electric switches.
    Statement B : We should play on the stairs.
    Which of the following is correct with respect to the above statements?
    (a) Statement A is correct
    (b) Statement B is correct
    (c) Both Statements A and B are correct
    (d) Neither statement A not statement B is correct

13. Match the following.

	Column I		Column II
A.	Red	1.	Wait
B.	Yellow	2.	Go
C.	Green	3.	Stop

    (a) A-3, B-1, C-2
    (b) A-2, B-1, C-3
    (c) A-3, B-1, C-2
    (d) A-1, B-3, C-2

14. If I sneeze, I would say.
    (a) Excuse me
    (b) Please
    (c) Thank You
    (d) Welcome
15. If my hands are wet, which one of the following, I should not touch?
    (a) Swimming tube
    (b) Torch
    (c) Toys
    (d) Electric switches
16. Which of the following should not be done once in a day?
    (a) Bath
    (b) Brushing teeth
    (c) Trim nails
    (d) Morning walk
17. Consider the following statements:
    Statement A : It is safe to play with knife.
    Statement B : We should play with medicine lying in the house.
    Which of the following is correct with respect to the above statements?
    (a) Statement A is correct
    (b) Statement B is correct
    (c) Both Statements A and B are correct
    (d) Neither statement A nor statement B is correct
18. When you do something wrong, you should say _____.
    (a) Sorry   (b) Thank You
    (c) Welcome   (d) Please
19. When your elder brother brings chocolate for you, you should say _____.
    (a) Sorry   (b) Thank You
    (c) Welcome   (d) Please
20. When you want to borrow a pencil from your friend, you should say _____.
    (a) Sorry   (b) Thank You
    (c) Welcome   (d) Please

ACHIEVERS SECTION

1. A new boy joined your class in the middle of the session. What kind of behavior should be shown by you?
   (a) You should bully him.
   (b) You should help him in completing his previous syllabus.
   (c) You should not talk to him.
   (d) You should ignore him. **[2018]**

2. Read the following rhyme and answer what is 'X' in the rhyme.

   X Light, X Light
   What do you say?
   I say go and go right away

(a) Red (b) Yellow
(c) Green (d) None of these

3. Which of the following options will replace 'X' and 'Y' in the Table.

Column I	Column II
'X'	
'Y'	

(a) X – Thank You, Y – Sorry
(b) X – Please, Y – Welcome
(c) X – Sorry, Y – Thank You
(d) X – Welcome, Y – Thank You

4. Match the following.

Column I		Column II	
A.	Play in	1.	Fire
B.	Walk on	2.	Zebra crossing
C.	Don't play with	3.	Playground
D.	Cross the road at	4.	Footpath

(a) A-4, B-3, C-1, D-2
(b) A-3, B-4, C-2, D-1
(c) A-3, B-4, C-1, D-2
(d) A-1, B-4, C-3, D-2

5. Some activities are given below
   1. Taking lunch
   2. Taking breakfast
   3. Brushing teeth
   4. Going to school

Please select the correct arrangement of these activities.

(a) 3, 4, 2, 1 (b) 1, 2, 3, 4
(c) 3, 2, 4, 1 (d) 3, 4, 1, 2

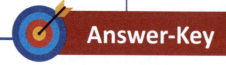

Answer-Key

LEVEL 1

1. (b)	2. (a)	3. (d)	4. (a)	5. (a)
6. (a)	7. (a)	8. (b)	9. (a)	10. (c)
11. (c)	12. (a)	13. (c)	14. (d)	15. (a)
16. (c)	17. (d)	18. (a)	19. (b)	20. (d)
21. (b)	22. (a)	23. (a)	24. (b)	25. (d)

Life Skills

LEVEL 2

1. (c)	2. (b)	3. (b)	4. (b)	5. (b)
6. (a)	7. (a)	8. (a)	9. (a)	10. (a)
11. (a)	12. (a)	13. (a)	14. (a)	15. (d)
16. (b)	17. (d)	18. (a)	19. (b)	20. (d)

ACHIEVERS SECTION

| 1. (b) | 2. (c) | 3. (c) | 4. (c) | 5. (c) |

Answers with Explanations

LEVEL 1

1. **Correct option is (b)**
   Explanation: Once you sit down, put the napkin on your lap to catch any food that falls.

2. **Correct option is (a)**
   Explanation: Don't play on the road as it can cause an accident.

3. **Correct option is (d)**
   Explanation: Pack your school bag for the next day → Brush your teeth → Read a book → Go to bed.

4. **Correct option is (a)**
   Explanation: Don't touch electric switches.
   Don't use sharp objects.
   Don't push others while getting into a bus.

5. **Correct option is (a)**
   Explanation: Pavement or footpath is a path for pedestrians at the side of a road. We should always walk on the pavement.

7. **Correct option is (a)**
   Explanation: Waking up early in the morning is a good habit as it makes us healthy.

8. **Correct option is (b)**
   Explanation: Footpath is a path for pedestrians at the side of a road.

9. **Correct option is (a)**
   Explanation: Combing hair, having breakfast and going to school, all these activities are done after brushing the teeth.

10. **Correct option is (c)**
    Explanation: Biting your nails is a bad habit as it can make you sick.

11. **Correct option is (c)**
    Explanation: Don't go deep into the water while swimming to avoid drowning.

13. **Correct option is (c)**

    Explanation: We should wash our hands before each meal to prevent infection.

14. **Correct option is (d)**

    Explanation: Fighting with others, eating junk food, throwing fruit peel on the road, these all are bad habits.

16. **Correct option is (c)**

    Explanation: Don't go deep into the water while swimming to avoid drowning.

17. **Correct option is (d)**

    Explanation: We should not rest our elbows on the table while eating as it is incredibly bad for our digestion.

18. **Correct option is (a)**

    Explanation: Washing your hands before eating a meal is a good habit because it prevents transmission of bacteria and germs from our hands to our mouth.

19. **Correct option is (b)**

    Explanation: Fighting with others is a bad habit. Instead we should work together to fix the issue.

20. **Correct option is (d)**

    Explanation: We go to school in the morning and lunch is taken in the noon.

21. **Correct option is (b)**

    Explanation: Sleeping very little is a bad habit as it damages our brain and makes us unhealthy.

23. **Correct option is (a)**

    Explanation: SLEEP WELL

24. **Correct option is (b)**

    Explanation: In the given picture, Suhan is sleeping, thus option (b) is correct.

25. **Correct option is (d)**

    Explanation: In the first picture, a girl is biting her nails which is a bad habit.

    In the second picture, a boy is washing his hands, which is a good habit.

    In the third picture, a boy is having junk food, which is a bad habit.

    In the fourth picture, a boy is sleeping to get enough sleep, which is a good habit.

LEVEL 2

1. **Correct option is (c)**

    Explanation: If there is too much dust in the air you breathe, cover your nose with a handkerchief, otherwise you will get infected.

2. **Correct option is (b)**

    Explanation: You will get hurt if you walk in front of swings when someone is swinging.

Life Skills

3. **Correct option is (b)**

   Explanation: Getting enough sleep is must to give rest to our body. It makes our body ready for another day.

4. **Correct option is (b)**

   Explanation: We should say thank you if someone help us. It is a way to show our appreciation to the person who helped us.

5. **Correct option is (b)**

   Explanation: We should share our things with others as it helps us to make and keep friends.

7. **Correct option is (a)**

   Explanation: Playing on stairs is not a good habit as you may slip and get hurt.

9. **Correct option is (a)**

   Explanation: Greeting guests with smile is a sign that guests are welcome. It also makes them comfortable.

10. **Correct option is (a)**

    Explanation: Saying thank you is a way to show that you appreciate their gift. It also makes them comfortable.

11. **Correct option is (a)**

    Explanation: Matchstick is used to light a fire.

12. **Correct option is (a)**

    Explanation: Playing with electric switches and playing on stairs, both are dangerous for us as we can get hurt if we do so.

13. **Correct option is (a)**

    Explanation:

    Red Light : Driver needs to stop

    Green light : Driver needs to start driving

    Yellow : Driver needs to slow down as the light is about to turn red

14. **Correct option is (a)**

    Explanation: After sneezing, we should say 'Excuse me'. When you say Excuse me, it means you are acknowledging that you have created inconvenience but it has to be done.

15. **Correct option is (d)**

    Explanation: We should not touch electric switches with wet hands as it increase the chances of getting electric shock.

16. **Correct option is (b)**

    Explanation: We should brush our teeth twice a day to prevent cavity.

18. **Correct option is (a)**

    Explanation: When you do something wrong, you should say sorry. It shows that you know it is your fault and you are feeling bad for it.

19. **Correct option is (b)**
    Explanation: Saying thank you is a way to show that you appreciate their gift. It also makes them happy.

20. **Correct option is (d)**
    Explanation: When you want to borrow a pencil from your friend, you should say please. It is a polite way to ask something or request for something.

ACHIEVERS SECTION

2. **Correct option is (c)**
   Explanation:
   Red Light: Stop
   Green light: Go
   Yellow: Wait

3. **Correct option is (c)**
   Explanation: You should say sorry, when you unknowingly hurt someone.

   You should say thank you, when someone gives you something or share their things with you.

4. **Correct option is (c)**

5. **Correct option is (c)**
   Explanation: Brushing Teeth → Taking Breakfast → Going to School → Taking Lunch

How to make learning
Fun, Effective & Responsive
at the same time?

It's easy!
Scan the QR codes below

Good Habits

Table Manners

Bad Habits

and get started!

Current Affairs

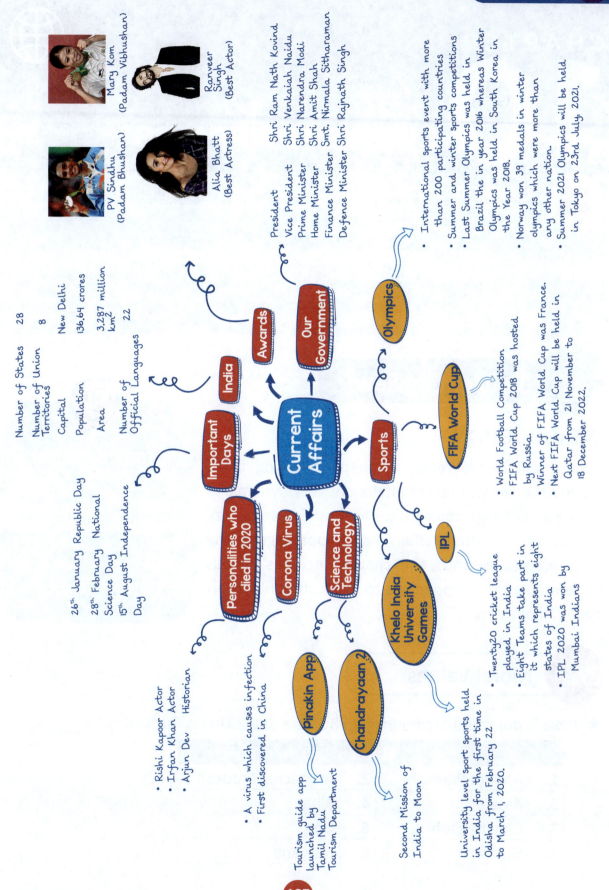

CHAPTER 10
CURRENT AFFAIRS

Learning Outcomes

Children would be able to:
- ✓ Know and recognize various Ministers of India;
- ✓ Know important days and their celebration;
- ✓ Know current affairs related to sports around the world;
- ✓ Know various awards and their winners.

Concept Review

INTRODUCTION

Current affairs are recent happenings taking place around the world. Current affairs are very dynamic in nature and change constantly. We should have quality knowledge of current affairs and happenings taking place around us. Thus, this chapter includes various current news and happenings to make students aware about all of them.

DID YOU KNOW?

According to the latest ranking of 2020 by Swachh Survekshan, Indore is the cleanest city and Surat is the second cleanest city of India.

Moral Values

★ India is our country comprising 28 States and 8 Union Territories.

	States		
1.	Andhra Pradesh	2.	Arunachal Pradesh
3.	Assam	4.	Bihar
5.	Chhattisgarh	6.	Goa
7.	Gujarat	8.	Haryana

188

Current Affairs

9.	Himachal Pradesh	10.	Jharkhand
11.	Karnataka	12.	Kerala
13.	Madhya Pradesh	14.	Maharashtra
15.	Manipur	16.	Meghalaya
17.	Mizoram	18.	Nagaland
19.	Odisha	20.	Punjab
21.	Rajasthan	22.	Sikkim
23.	Tamil Nadu	24.	Telangana
25.	Tripura	26.	Uttar Pradesh
27.	Uttarakhand	28.	West Bengal

DID YOU KNOW?

Joe Biden is the current President of USA.

Union Territories				
1.	Andaman and Nicobar Islands	5.	Jammu and Kashmir
2.	Chandigarh	6.	Lakshadweep
3.	Dadra & Nagar Haveli and Daman & Diu	7.	Puducherry
4.	Delhi	8.	Ladakh

DID YOU KNOW?

The Governor of the Reserve Bank of India is Shri Shaktikanta Das.

In 2019, Jammu and Kashmir reconstituted into two Union Territories, one designated as Jammu and Kashmir and the other as Ladakh.

★ **Our Government:**

Who's Who	
President	Shri Ram Nath Kovind
Vice President	Shri Venkaiah Naidu
Prime Minister	Shri Narendra Modi
Defence Minister	Shri Rajnath Singh

189

Home Minister	Shri Amit Shah	
Finance Minister	Smt. Nirmala Sitharaman	
Education Minister	Shri Ramesh Pokhriyal 'Nishank'	
Chief Minister of Uttar Pradesh	Shri Yogi Adityanath	
Chief Minister of Delhi	Shri Arvind Kejriwal	

★ **Important Days**

1. **Independence Day:** On 15th August 1947, India got freedom from the British rule and since then this day is celebrated as Independence Day throughout the country. India has proudly celebrated 74th Independence Day on 15th August, 2020.

2. **Republic Day:** Republic Day is celebrated annually on 26th January. On the same day in 1950, our Constitution came into effect. India has proudly celebrated 71st Republic Day on 26th January, 2020. The chief guest for 71st Republic Day was the President of Brazil, Jair Messias Bolsonaro.

3. **National Science Day:** National Science Day is celebrated on 28th February each year across the country as on this same day, the discovery of Raman Effect was announced by Sir CV Raman. He got Nobel Prize in 1930 for this discovery. Theme for National Science Day, 2020 was "Women in Science" and for 2021 is "Future of STI: Impacts on Education, Skills and Work".

Current Affairs

★ **Sports**

1. **FIFA World Cup:**
   - FIFA World Cup is the most prestigious Football competition in the world.
   - It is played in every four years.
   - Last FIFA World Cup was hosted in 2018 by Russia. It was won by France.
   - Next FIFA World Cup is scheduled to be held in Qatar from 21th November to 18th December 2022.

DID YOU KNOW?
India finished year 2019 as the top shooting nation in the world.

2. **Olympics:**
   - The Olympic Games are considered to be the world's best athletic competition with more than 200 participating countries.
   - Last Summer Olympics was held in Brazil in the year 2016.
   - Winter Olympics was held in South Korea in year 2018. In this, Norway won 39 medals which were more than any other nation.
   - The 2020 Summer Olympics have been postponed due to the COVID-19 epidemic. Now it has been scheduled on 23rd July, 2021.

3. **IPL:**
   - It is the Twenty20 cricket league.
   - It is generally held between March and May each year.
   - Eight states of India representing eight teams take part in it every year.
   - The last IPL that was IPL 2020, was won by Mumbai Indians.

4. **Wimbledon Championship:**
   - It is the oldest tennis tournament of the world.
   - It has been held at the All England Club in Wimbledon, London since 1877.
   - The winners of Wimbledon Championship 2019 are:

Wimbledon Titles	Wimbledon Winners
Wimbledon 2019 Gentlemen's Singles	Novak Djokovic
Wimbledon 2019 Ladies Singles	Simona Halep

   - The Wimbledon Championship, 2020 has been postponed due to Corona Virus Disease and will begin on 28th May, 2021.

5. **Khelo India University Games:**
   - It is the national sporting event held in India.
   - It is the largest competition ever held at university level in India.
   - The first edition of this competition held in Odisha started on February 22 and ended on March 1, 2020.

DID YOU KNOW?
Miss World 2019 is Toni-Ann Singh and Miss Universe 2020 is Zozibini Tunzi.

★ **Awards 2020**

Awards	Winner
Padam Vibhushan	MC Mary Kom (Sports)
Padam Bhushan	PV Sindhu (Sports)
National Filmfare Award -Best Film	Gully Boy
National Filmfare Award Best Actor	Ranveer Singh
National Filmfare Award Best Actress	Alia Bhatt
Dadasaheb Phalke Award	Dhanush K Raja

★ **Science and Technology**
  1. **Pinakin App:** Pinakin App has been launched recently by the Tamil Nadu Tourism Department which provides information as a guide on major tourist destinations in South India.
  2. **Chandrayaan-2:** It is second mission of India to Moon launched on 22nd July 2019 by the Indian Space Research Organisation, after Chandrayaan-1.

★ **CORONA Virus**

Corona Virus causes infection caused by socializing. It was firstly identified in Wuhan, China. It primarily affects our respiratory system and damages it. To prevent it from spreading, we should wash our hands with soap for approx. 20 seconds and follow social distancing. It is also known as Covid-19 which stands for 'Corona Virus Disease 2019'.

Current Affairs

Multiple Choice Questions

LEVEL 1

1. Who is the winner of 2019 Men's Singles Wimbledon Championship?

   (a)
   Roger Federer

   (b)
   Novak Djokovic

   (c)
   Nadal

   (d)
   Andy Marray   **[2019]**

2. Who is the current Finance Minister of India?

   (a)
   Arun Jaitely

   (b)
   Nirmala Sitharaman

   (c)
   Nitish Kumar

   (d) None of these   **[2019]**

3. _____ is India's second mission to Moon.
   (a) Chandrayaan-1
   (b) Apollo-11
   (c) Chandrayaan-2
   (d) Apollo-7   **[2019]**

4. The winner of ICC Cricket World Cup 2019 is _____ .
   (a) India
   (b) West Indies
   (c) England
   (d) South Africa   **[2019]**

5. Who is the Prime Minister of India?

   (a)
   Ram Nath Kovind

(b)
Venkaiah Naidu

(c)
Narendra Modi

(d) None of these. **[2019]**

6. Who is the current President of India?

(a)
Narendra Modi

(b)
Arvind Kejriwal

(c)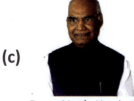
Ram Nath Kovind

(d) None of these **[2018]**

7. On which day do we celebrate the Republic Day?
   (a) 26th January
   (b) 15th August
   (c) 2nd October
   (d) 22nd March **[2018]**

8. 'Jurassic World: _____' is a famous movie released in 2018. Complete the name of this movie.
   (a) Fallen Kingdom
   (b) The Lost World
   (c) Isla Nublar
   (d) Velociraptor **[2018]**

9. Which country is the winner of FIFA World Cup 2018?
   (a) Croatia
   (b) France
   (c) Russia
   (d) Spain **[2018]**

10. What is the professional Twenty20 cricket league in India called?
    (a) IPL
    (b) World Cup
    (c) Big Bash League
    (d) None of these

11. The Corona virus has originated from which country?
    (a) America
    (b) India
    (c) China
    (d) Italy

12. What does Covid-19 stand for?
    (a) Corona Virus Disease 2019
    (b) Covid-2019
    (c) Co-Virus – 2019
    (d) Corona Virus - 19

13. How long you should wash your hands?
    (a) 5 seconds   (b) 20 seconds
    (c) 1 minute   (d) 1 hour
14. Social distancing can help prevent corona virus.
    (a) True
    (b) False
    (c) Both (a) and (b)
    (d) Neither (a) nor (b)
15. Where was the IPL 2020 held?
    (a) United States of America
    (b) United Arab Emirates
    (c) India
    (d) China
16. How many teams participated in IPL 2020?
    (a) 6   (b) 7
    (d) 4   (d) 8
17. Which team won IPL 2020?
    (a) Mumbai Indians
    (b) Chennai Super Kings
    (c) Delhi Capitals
    (d) Rajasthan Royals
18. When did IPL 2020 start?
    (a) 1 January, 2020
    (b) 19 September, 2020
    (c) 10 November, 2020
    (d) None of these
19. Who is the current President of United States of America?
    (a) Donald Trump
    (b) Barack Obama
    (c) Joe Biden
    (d) George W. Bush
20. _____ was recently awarded the Padma Vibhushan in 2020 for her efforts in the Olympics.
    (a) Sania Mirza
    (b) PV Sindhu
    (c) Kalpana Chawla
    (d) Mary Kom
21. Where did the 2018 Winter Olympics held?
    (a) South Korea
    (b) United States of America
    (c) Japan
    (d) India
22. How many countries participated in the 2018 Winter Olympics?
    (a) 83   (b) 92
    (c) 74   (d) 105
23. Where will the 2022 winter Olympics be held?
    (a) United States of America
    (b) India
    (c) South Korea
    (d) Beijing
24. Where was the Summer Olympics 2020 held?
    (a) Japan   (b) France
    (b) South Korea (d) India
25. Which country won the most Olympic medals in 2018?
    (a) Norway
    (b) Italy
    (c) Japan
    (d) China

26. What was the official mascot of Winter Olympics 2018?

(a)

(b)

(c)

(d)

27. What was the motto of Olympics 2020?
    (a) Play for fun
    (b) Do and win
    (c) Discover Tomorrow
    (d) None of these

28. When do we celebrate Independence Day?
    (a) 26th January   (b) 15th August
    (c) 14th November   (d) 5th September

29. How many states are there in India?
    (a) 26   (b) 27
    (c) 28   (d) 29

30. Who is the current Chief Minister of Delhi?

(a)
Yogo Aditya Nath

(b)
Arvind Kejriwal

(c)
Narendra Modi

(d)
Nitish Kumar

31. Who among the following won the 2019 Miss World Competition?

(a)
Zozibini Tunzi

(b)
Toni-Ann Singh

Current Affairs

(c)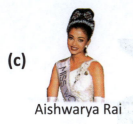
Aishwarya Rai

(d)
Vanessa Ponce

32. Who is the current Governor of Reserve Bank of India (RBI)?

(a)
Shaktikanta Das

(b)
Urjit Patel

(c)
Duvvuri Subbarao

(d) None of these

33. Irfan Khan who passed away recently was a _____.

(a) Singer
(b) Actor
(c) Painter
(d) Dancer

34. Chandrayaan-2 is India's _____ mission to Moon.

(a) First
(b) Second
(c) Third
(d) Forth

35. Who received the best actor award in Film Fare Awards 2020?

(a)
Shahrukh Khan

(b)
Salman Khan

(c)
Ayushman Khurana

(d)
Ranveer Singh

36. Who received the best actress award in Film Fare Awards 2020?

(a)
Deepika Padukone

(b)
Keerthy Suresh

(c)
Alia Bhatt

(d)
Kriti Senon

37. Arjun Dev who passed away in March 2020 was a/an _____.
    (a) Actor   (b) Painter
    (c) Singer   (d) Historian

38. Name the actor who passed away in April 2020?

(a)
Firoz Khan

(b)
Amrish Puri

(c)
Om Puri

(d)
Rishi Kapoor

39. Which of the following states in India has been reconstituted into two Union Territories in 2019?
    (a) Andhra Pradesh
    (b) Jammu and Kashmir
    (c) Tamil Nadu
    (d) Uttarakhand

40. Which country will host FIFA World Cup 2022?
    (a) France
    (b) India
    (c) Qatar
    (d) United States of America

Current Affairs

41. Who was crowned Miss Universe 2019?

(a) Zozibini Tunzi

(b) Toni-Ann Singh

(c) Aishwarya Rai

(d) Vanessa Ponce

42. Which Badminton World Champion has been awarded the Padam Bhushan?
    (a) Mary Kom
    (b) P V Sindhu
    (c) Sania Mirza
    (d) Saina Nehwal

43. Pinakin Mobile App was launched by which state tourism department to boost tourism?
    (a) Karnataka
    (b) Tamil Nadu
    (c) Bihar
    (d) Mumbai

44. Who is the Vice President of India?
    (a) Ramnath Kovind
    (b) Rajnath Singh
    (c) Amit Shah
    (d) Venkaiah Naidu

45. The first edition of _____ is scheduled to be held at the KIIT University in Bhubaneswar from February 22 to March 1, 2020.
    (a) Khelo India University Games
    (b) Indian Wrestling Championship
    (c) Indian Ice Hockey League
    (d) None of these

46. _____ finished the year as the top shooting nation in the world.
    (a) USA
    (b) China
    (c) India
    (d) Russia

47. Who is the current Home Minister of India?

(a) Amit Shah

(b) Nirmala Sitharaman

(c)

(d) None of these

48. Who is the current Education Minister of India?

(a)
Amit Shah

(b)
Nirmala Sitharaman

(c)

(d) None of these

49. Who was the chief guest at the Republic Day parade of India, 2020?
    (a) The President of Brazil
    (b) The President of USA
    (c) The President of South Africa
    (d) The Prime Minister of Bangladesh

50. Which city in India has been declared as the cleanest city by Swachh Survekshan Report in 2020?
    (a) Bhopal   (b) Chandigarh
    (c) Indore   (d) Mysore

Answer-Key

LEVEL 1

1. (b)	2. (b)	3. (c)	4. (c)	5. (c)
6. (c)	7. (a)	8. (a)	9. (b)	10. (a)
11. (c)	12. (a)	13. (b)	14. (a)	15. (b)
16. (d)	17. (a)	18. (b)	19. (c)	20. (d)
21. (a)	22. (b)	23. (d)	24. (a)	25. (a)
26. (c)	27. (d)	28. (b)	29. (c)	30. (b)
31. (b)	32. (a)	33. (b)	34. (b)	35. (d)
36. (c)	37. (d)	38. (d)	39. (b)	40. (c)
41. (a)	42. (b)	43. (b)	44. (d)	45. (a)
46. (c)	47. (a)	48. (c)	49. (a)	50. (c)

Current Affairs

Answers with Explanations

LEVEL 1

1. **Correct option is (b)**
   Explanation : Novak Djokovic won Men's Singles Wimbledon Championship, 2019 by defeating Rojer Federer.

2. **Correct option is (b)**
   Explanation : Smt. Nirmala Sitharaman took charge from 31st May, 2019 as the Finance Minister of India.

3. **Correct option is (c)**
   Explanation : Chandrayaan-2 is second Mission of India to Moon, launched by ISRO (Indian Space Research Organisation) on 22nd July, 2019.

4. **Correct option is (c)**
   Explanation : England won ICC World Cup 2019 by defeating New Zealand.

5. **Correct option is (c)**
   Explanation : Narendra Modi is the Prime Minister of India since 2014.

6. **Correct option is (c)**
   Explanation: Ram Nath Kovind took oath on 25th July 2017 as India's 14th President.

7. **Correct option is (a)**
   Explanation: The Constitution of India came into force on 26th January, 1950.

9. **Correct option is (b)**
   Explanation : France won the FIFA World Cup 2018 by defeating Croatia.

10. **Correct option is (a)**
    Explanation : The Indian Premier League is the 20-20 cricket league played in India which is generally held between March and May each year.

11. **Correct option is (c)**
    Explanation : Corona Virus causing Covid-19 was first identified in Wuhan city of China.

12. **Correct option is (a)**
    Explanation : CO-Corona
    Vi-Virus
    D-Disease
    19-2019

15. **Correct option is (b)**
    Explanation: The Indian Premier League, 2020 was held in the United Arab Emirates (UAE) from September 19 to November 10.

16. **Correct option is (d)**
    Explanation: Eight teams participated in IPL 2020 which were Chennai Super Kings, Mumbai Indians, Kolkata Knight Riders,

Sunrisers Hyderabad, Rajasthan Royals, Kings XI Punjab, Royal Challengers Bangalore, and Delhi Capitals.

17. **Correct option is (a)**

    Explanation: Mumbai Indians won IPL 2020 Final by defeating Delhi Capitals.

18. **Correct option is (b)**

    Explanation: The Indian Premier League, 2020 was held in the United Arab Emirates (UAE), started from September 19 and ended on November 10.

19. **Correct option is (c)**

    Explanation: Joe Biden is the 46th and current President of America. He took his oath as President of United States on 20th January, 2021.

20. **Correct option is (d)**

    Explanation: Mary Kom, an Indian Boxer, was awarded Padam Vibhushan. It is the second-highest civilian award of India.

21. **Correct option is (a)**

    Explanation: Winter Olympics, 2018 was held at the Pyeongchang Olympic Stadium in South Korea on 9th February 2018.

23. **Correct option is (d)**

    Explanation: 2022 Winter Olympics will begin on 4th February, 2022 in Beijing, China.

24. **Correct option is (a)**

    Explanation: Summer Olympics, 2020 will begin on 23rd July 2021 in Tokyo, Japan.

25. **Correct option is (a)**

    Explanation: In Winter Olympics 2018, Norway won 39 medals which were more than any other nation.

28. **Correct option is (b)**

    Explanation: On 15th August 1947, India got freedom from the British rule and since then this day is celebrated as Independence Day throughout the country.

29. **Correct option is (c)**

    Explanation: India has 28 states and 8 union territories as on January 2021.

30. **Correct option is (b)**

    Explanation: Arvind Kejriwal is 7th Chief Minister of Delhi since February 2015.

31. **Correct option is (b)**

    Explanation: Toni-Ann Singh was crowned Miss World 2019 at an annual beauty pageant held in London on 14th December, 2019.

32. **Correct option is (a)**

    Explanation: Shaktikanta Das is the 25th Governor of RBI and took his charge on 12th December, 2018.

33. **Correct option is (b)**

Explanation: Irfan Khan was an Indian actor who passed away on 29th April, 2020 due to colon infection.

34. **Correct option is (b)**
    Explanation: Chandrayaan-2 is the second mission of India to Moon, launched on 22nd July 2019, by the Indian Space Research Organisation.

35. **Correct option is (d)**
    Explanation: Ranveer Singh was awarded with Best Actor Filmfare Award for the movie, 'Gully Boy'.

36. **Correct option is (c)**
    Explanation: Alia Bhatt was awarded with Best Actress Filmfare Award for the movie, 'Gully Boy'.

37. **Correct option is (d)**
    Explanation: Prof. Arjun Dev, eminent historian and educationist, passed away on March 29, at the age of 82.

38. **Correct option is (d)**
    Explanation: Rishi Kapoor, an Indian actor, passed away on 30th April, 2020 due to the disease, Leukemia.

39. **Correct option is (b)**
    Explanation: Jammu and Kashmir in India has been reconstituted into two Union Territories, viz. Jammu and Kashmir and Ladakh as per Jammu and Kashmir Reorganisation Act, 2019 that came into effect on October 31, 2019.

42. **Correct option is (b)**
    Explanation: PV Sindhu, an Indian Badminton player, was awarded with Padam Bhushan, second highest civilian award of India, in 2020.

43. **Correct option is (b)**
    Explanation: Pinakin App has been launched recently by the Tamil Nadu Tourism Department which provides information as a guide on major tourist destinations in South India.

44. **Correct option is (d)**
    Explanation: Venkaiah Naidu is the current Vice President of India, since 11 August, 2017.

45. **Correct option is (a)**
    Explanation: Khelo India University Games (KIUG), the national sporting event held in India, is the largest competition ever held at university level in India. The first edition of this competition held in Odisha started on February 22 and ended on March 1, 2020.

47. **Correct option is (a)**
    Explanation: Amit Shah is the current Home Minister of India and took his charge from June 21, 2020.

49. **Correct option is (a)**

Explanation: The President of Brazil, Jair Messias Bolsonaro, was the chief guest at India's 71st Republic Day Parade on January 26.

50. **Correct option is (c)**

    Explanation: Indore won the award for India's cleanest city for the fourth consecutive year.

How to make learning
Fun, Effective & Responsive
at the same time?

It's easy!
Scan the QR codes below

Places of Worship   Current Affairs 2020

and get started!

LEVEL 1 SAMPLE QUESTION PAPER

Total Marks: 40   Total Questions: 35   Total Time: 1 Hr

General Instructions

(i) All questions are compulsory.
(ii) Calculators, log tables and other aids are not permitted.
(iii) The question paper has two sections.
  (1) Multiple Choice Questions; has 30 questions, each carries 1 mark.
  (2) Achievers Section; has 5 questions, each carries 2 marks.
(iv) There is no negative marking.
(v) Correct options should be clearly filled in separate Answer Sheet.

Multiple Choice Questions

LEVEL 1

1. Fill in the blank with the help of the picture.

   Ravi is _____.
   (a) happy   (b) sad
   (c) afraid   (d) surprised

2. Find the odd one out.
   (a) Parents
   (b) Siblings
   (c) Grandfather
   (d) Friends

3. Which part of our body helps us to hear different sounds?
   (a) Ears
   (b) Teeth
   (c) Eyes
   (d) Hands

4. _____ is present in the chest.

   (a)   (b)

   (c)   (d)

5. Which of the following fruits contain only one seed?

(a)   (b)

(c)   (d)

6. Which of the following is not a part of plant?
   (a) Root   (b) Stem
   (c) Leaf   (d) Herb

7. Which one is not an aquatic animal?

(a)   (b)

(c)   (d)

8. Match the Column I and Column II.

Column I		Column II	
A.	Dog	1.	Den
B.	Fox	2.	Shed
C.	Bird	3.	Kennel
D.	Cow	4.	Nest

   (a) A-3, B-1, C-4, D-2
   (b) A-4, B-1, C-2, D-3
   (c) A-3, B-4, C-1, D-2
   (d) A-1, B-3, C-4, D-2

9. Identify the national animal of India.

(a)   (b)

(c)   (d)

10. Which of the following statement is true?
    (a) Dog is a wild animal.
    (b) Cow gives us milk.
    (c) Rabbit lives in water.
    (d) Lion helps in transportation.

11. Identify the name of young one of the given animal.

    (a) Cub   (b) Lamb
    (c) Joey   (d) Kid

12. Identify the festival related to the picture shown.

    (a) Eid   (b) Diwali
    (c) Christmas (d) Gurpurab

13. Which day is celebrated on 5th September?
    (a) Children's Day
    (b) Teacher's Day
    (c) Independence Day
    (d) National Science Day

14. Who among the following is known as 'Father of the Nation'?
    (a) Mahatma Gandhi
    (b) Lal Krishna Advani
    (c) Jawahar Lal Nehru
    (d) APJ Abdul Kalam

15. 'Leaning Tower of Pisa' is located in _____.
    (a) London   (b) China
    (c) Italy   (d) Chicago

16. Look at the given pictures carefully and select the odd one out.

    (a)   (b)

    (c)   (d)

17. The object shown in the picture is a commonly used device. What is it?

    (a) Electric Iron
    (b) Microwave oven
    (c) Toaster
    (d) Vacuum Cleaner

18. Choose the odd one out.
    (a) Volleyball   (b) Hockey
    (c) Golf   (d) Carrom

19. The author of book the 'Harry Potter' is _____.
    (a) J. K. Rowling
    (b) Shakespeare
    (c) Barack Obama
    (d) Sachin Tendulkar

20. How many triangles are given in the below figure?

    (a) 6   (b) 7
    (d) 5   (c) 8

21. Who is standing at fourth position from the left?

    (a) Hattori   (b) Tom
    (c) Doraemon   (d) Aladdin

22. Who is the current Prime Minister of India?

    (a)   (b)

    (c)   (d)

23. Tokyo Olympics has been canceled for how many years because of COVID-19?
    (a) 1 year   (b) 2 years
    (c) 3 years   (d) 4 years

24. Recognize this actor:

   (a) Amitabh Bachchan
   (b) Shahrukh Khan
   (c) Salman Khan
   (d) Akshay Kumar

25. This monument is located in _____.

   (a) Agra   (b) Delhi
   (c) Amritsar   (d) Kolkata

26. My father's son is my _____.
   (a) Cousin   (b) Brother
   (c) Uncle   (d) Grandfather

27. Which of the following is not a means of transportation?

   (a)   (b)
   (c)   (d)

28. Match the rhyming words.

Column I		Column II	
A.	Cap	1.	Win
B.	Pin	2.	Band
C.	Sand	3.	Hook
D.	Book	4.	Map

   (a) A-4, B-1, C-2, D-3
   (b) A-3, B-1, C-2, D-4
   (c) A-2, B-1, C-4, D-3
   (d) A-2, B-3, C-1, D-4

29. Which of the following is not a part of computer?
   (a) Monitor   (b) Rat
   (c) Keyboard   (d) CPU

30. Give a group name for the following set of words.

   > cards, dogs, hyenas, lies, wolves, hounds

   (a) Herd   (b) Pack
   (c) Flock   (d) Gang

ACHIEVERS SECTION

Read the following rhyme and answer the questions from 1-3.

Hickory, dickory, dock.
The mouse ran up the clock.
The clock struck one,
The mouse ran down,
Hickory, dickory, dock.

1. Who ran up the clock?
   (a) Mouse   (b) Cat
   (c) Lion   (d) Horse

2. At what time did the clock strike?
   (a) 1:00   (b) 3:00
   (c) 12:00   (d) 5:00

Sample Question Paper, Level-1

3. What did the mouse do when the clock struck one?
   (a) Ran up
   (b) Ran down
   (c) Get in
   (d) None of the above

4. Find the missing number in the given pattern.

   (a) 12   (b) 14
   (c) 13   (d) 10

5. Which of the following options shows the correct amount of money as the cost of the given ball?

   (a)
   (b)
   (c)
   (d)

 Answer-Key

LEVEL 1

1. (a)	2. (d)	3. (a)	4. (a)	5. (c)
6. (d)	7. (d)	8. (a)	9. (a)	10. (b)
11. (b)	12. (b)	13. (b)	14. (a)	15. (c)
16. (d)	17. (d)	18. (d)	19. (a)	20. (b)
21. (a)	22. (a)	23. (a)	24. (b)	25. (b)
26. (b)	27. (d)	28. (a)	29. (b)	30. (b)

ACHIEVERS SECTION

| 1. (a) | 2. (a) | 3. (b) | 4. (b) | 5. (a) |

Answers with Explanations

LEVEL 1

2. Correct option is (d)
Explanation: Parents, grandparents and siblings are the parts of a family.

4. Correct option is (a)
Explanation: The heart is located in the chest between the lungs but to the left of the center.

5. Correct option is (c)
Explanation: An apple has around 5 seeds. A papaya has around 115 seeds. A watermelon has between 300 -500 seeds.

6. Correct option is (d)
Explanation: Herb is a type of plant.

7. Correct option is (d)
Explanation: Lion is a terrestrial animal.

9. Correct option is (a)
Explanation: Tiger is the national animal of India as it is a symbol of grace, strength, agility and enormous power.

10. Correct option is (b)
Explanation: Dog is a domestic animal. Rabbit is a terrestrial animal as it lives on land. Lion is a wild animal and cannot be tamed for the help of humans.

11. Correct option is (b)
Explanation:

Animals	Young Ones
Lion	Cub
Sheep	Lamb
Kangaroo	Joey
Goat	Kid

12. Correct option is (b)
Explanation: Diwali is a festival of lights. We decorate our home with candles, earthen lamps and lights. Children enjoy with their friends by burning firecrackers.

13. Correct option is (b)
Explanation: We celebrate Teacher's Day on 5th September annually to honor the contribution made by teachers to our society. 5th September is the birth date of Dr. Sarvepalli Radhakrishnan who was a scholar, teacher, and politician and dictated his life towards education.

15. Correct option is (c)
Explanation:

Places	Famous Monuments
London	Big Ben
China	Great Wall of China
Italy	Leaning Tower of Pisa
Chicago	Millennium Park

16. Correct option is (d)
Explanation: Shoes are made of leather, where as mug, bottle, and container are made of plastic.

17. Correct option is (d)
Explanation: Vacuum cleaner is used to clean our house as it sucks up dust and dirt.

18. **Correct option is (d)**
    Explanation: Volleyball, hockey, and golf are outdoor games whereas, carrom is an indoor game.

19. **Correct option is (a)**
    Explanation: J. K. Rowling is a famous British author, who wrote the book, 'Harry Potter'.

21. **Correct option is (a)**
    Explanation:

Position	From Left	From Right
1st	Chhota Bheem	Mickey Mouse
2nd	Doraemon	Aladdin
3rd	Tom	Hattori
4th	Hattori	Tom
5th	Aladdin	Doraemon
6th	Mickey Mouse	Chhota Bheem

22. **Correct option is (a)**
    Explanation: Image given in the option:
    (a) is of Shri Narendra Modi, who is the current Prime Minister of India.
    (b) is of Shri Rajnath Singh, who is the current Defence Minister of India.
    (c) is of Shri Ramnath Kovind, who is the current President of India.
    (d) is of Shri Manmohan Singh, who was the 13th Prime Minister of India.

23. **Correct option is (a)**
    Explanation: The 2020 Summer Olympics have been postponed for a year due to the COVID-19 pandemic. Now it has been scheduled on 23rd July, 2021.

25. **Correct option is (b)**
    Explanation:

Places	Famous Monuments
Agra	Taj Mahal
Delhi	Red Fort
Amritsar	Golden Temple
Kolkata	Victoria Memorial

26. **Correct option is (b)**
    Explanation:

    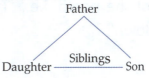

27. **Correct option is (d)**
    Explanation: Television is an electronic device and a mode of mass communication.

28. **Correct option is (a)**
    Explanation: 'Cap' and 'Map' are ending with an identical sound. 'Pin' and 'Win' are ending with an identical sound. 'Sand' and 'Band' are ending with an identical sound. 'Book' and 'Hook' are ending with an identical sound.

29. **Correct option is (b)**
    Explanation: Monitor is a display unit which shows all the work which is going on inside the computer.
    Keyboard is an input unit used to enter work into the computer.
    CPU is the brain of computer as it stores all the information.

ACHIEVERS SECTION

1. **Correct option is (a)**
   Explanation: It is stated in the 2nd line of the poem, i.e., 'The mouse ran up the clock'.

2. **Correct option is (a)**
   Explanation: It is stated in the 3rd line of the poem, i.e., 'The clock struck one'.

3. **Correct option is (b)**
   Explanation: It is stated in the 4th line of the poem, i.e., 'The mouse ran down'.

4. **Correct option is (b)**
   Explanation:
   $2 \xrightarrow{+3} 5 \xrightarrow{+3} 8 \xrightarrow{+3} 11 \xrightarrow{+3} 14 \xrightarrow{+3} 17$

5. **Correct option is (a)**
   Explanation:
   Option (a): 100+20+5 = 125
   Option (b): 200+20+5 = 225
   Option (c): 100+10+5 = 115
   Option (d): 100+10+10 = 120

LEVEL 2 SAMPLE QUESTION PAPER

Total Marks: 60 Total Questions: 50 Total Time: 1 Hr

General Instructions

(i) All questions are compulsory.
(ii) Calculators, log tables and other aids are not permitted.
(iii) The question paper has two sections.
   (1) Multiple Choice Questions; has 45 questions, each carries 1 mark.
   (2) Achievers Section; has 5 questions, each carries 3 marks.
(iv) There is no negative marking.
(v) Correct options should be clearly filled in separate Answer Sheet.

Multiple Choice Questions

LEVEL 2

1. Rahul is Mr. Rakesh's son and Ashok is Mr. Rakesh's brother. What is the relation of Rahul with Ashok?
   (a) Mother (b) Uncle
   (c) Friend (d) Grand Father

2. There is a nuclear family, who has 3 children. Akshay is the eldest. Next is Ravi. The last child in the family is a girl, Amita. How is Amita related to Akshay?
   (a) Sister (b) Cousin
   (c) Mother (d) Aunt

3. Which of the following is an incorrect match?

	Column I	Column II
(a)	See	
(b)	Hear	
(c)	Touch	
(d)	Taste	

4. Who am I?

(a) Doctor (b) Nurse
(c) Plumber (d) Soldier

5. Unscramble the word given below.

dlhosure

(a) Should (b) Scapular
(c) Allowed (d) Shoulder

6. _____ holds plant firmly in place.
(a) Root (b) Stem
(c) Leaf (d) Fruit

7. Which of the following is a herb?
(a) Tulsi
(b) Banyan
(c) Pumpkin
(d) Money plant

8. Which of the following options replaces 'X' and 'Y' in the following.

Wild Animal	Lion	Fox
Domestic Animal	'X'	Dog
Birds	Parrot	'Y'

(a) X-Eagle, Y-Cow
(b) X-Vulture, Y-Pigeon
(c) X-Cat, Y-Butterfly
(d) X-Cow, Y-Peacock

9. Which of the following is not true about plants?
(a) Plants give us fruits.
(b) Plants have leaves.
(c) Stem of plant grows above the surface.
(d) Plants can move from one place to another.

10. _____ changes into fruits.
(a) Seeds (b) Flowers
(c) Leaves (d) Stem

11. Consider the following statements and choose the correct answer.
Statement A: Wheat and sunflower are the examples of herbs.
Statement B: Climbers grow along the ground.
Statement C: Papaya is an example of flower.
(a) Statement A is true and B, C are false.
(b) Statement A, B are true and C is false.
(c) All are true.
(d) All are false.

12. How many names of animals are hidden in the given word grid?

G	P	T	H	L	I	O	N
M	O	N	K	E	Y	D	S
O	R	O	S	Q	L	W	Z
N	C	N	H	G	S	D	E
G	A	D	O	J	H	P	B
O	H	O	R	S	E	O	K
R	L	G	L	K	E	L	E
T	M	B	I	C	P	X	N

(a) 4 (b) 5
(c) 6 (d) 7

Sample Question Paper, Level-2

13. The archway shown in the picture is situated in Agra. What is it called?

   (a) Gateway of India
   (b) India Gate
   (c) Taj Mahal
   (d) Golden Temple

14. Which of the following statement is not true about the given image?

   (a) It is a festival of lights.
   (b) Homes are decorated with earthen lamps.
   (c) People prepare seviyan.
   (d) Both (a) and (b)

15. Match the items in column I with column II and choose the correct answer from the given options.

	Column I		Column II
A.	Independence Day	1.	5th September
B.	Republic Day	2.	14th November
C.	Teacher's Day	3.	15th August
D.	Children's Day	4.	26th January

   (a) A-4, B-3, C-1, D-2
   (b) A-3, B-4, C-2, D-1
   (c) A-3, B-1, C-4, D-2
   (d) A-3, B-4, C-1, D-2

16. Who wrote India's national song 'Vande Mataram'?
   (a) Rabindra Nath Tagore
   (b) Bankim Chandra Chatterjee
   (c) Jawahar Lal Nehru
   (d) Mahatma Gandhi

17. Select the odd one out from the given group.

   Refrigerator, Washing Machine, Vacuum Cleaner, Table

   (a) Table
   (b) Refrigerator
   (c) Washing Machine
   (d) Vacuum Cleaner

18. Which sport is being played in the picture?

   (a) Volleyball   (b) Basketball
   (c) Hockey   (d) Cricket

19. What is the lowest number you can get by throwing a single dice?
   (a) 1   (b) 3
   (c) 6   (d) 2

20. Which of the following princess stuck her finger in a spinning wheel?
   (a) Snow White (b) Cinderella
   (c) Aurora   (d) Goldilocks

21. Match the following.

	Column I		Column II
A.	Playing It My Way	1.	Chetan Bhagat
B.	My Music My Life	2.	Sachin Tendulkar
C.	Discovery of India	3.	Pandit Ravi Shankar
D.	Making India Awesome	4.	Pandit Jawaharlal Nehru

(a) A-2, B-3, C-4, D-1
(b) A-3, B-2, C-4, D-1
(c) A-2, B-4, C-3, D-1
(d) A-2, B-3, C-1, D-4

22. Next figure in the given figure pattern is _____.

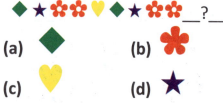

(a) ◆ (b) ✿
(c) ♥ (d) ★

23. If Parul's birthday is on Friday of May, 2021, identify the date when she will not celebrate his birthday definitely.

(a) 7th May (b) 14th May
(c) 22nd May (d) 28th May

24. Third girl from the left is _____.

(a) Maria (b) Hana
(c) Candy (d) Shaka

25. 3 hundreds + 7 tens + 9 ones = ____
(a) 379 (b) 973
(c) 739 (d) 397

26. Who is the winner of 2019 Women's Singles Wimbledon Championships?
(a) Simona Halep
(b) Serena Williams
(c) Maria Sharapova
(d) Saina Nehwal

27. Who is the current Defence Minister of India?
(a) Ramnath Kovind
(b) Rajnath Singh
(c) Narendra Modi
(d) Nirmala Sitharaman

28. Chandrayaan-2 is India's_____ mission to Moon.
(a) First (b) Second
(c) Third (d) Forth

29. I always say _____, when I get a gift.
(a) Sorry (b) Thank You
(c) Welcome (d) Please

30. Consider the following two statements.
   Statement A: We should push others to go ahead.
   Statement B: We should not throw rubbish on the road.
(a) Statement A is correct.
(b) Statement B is correct.
(c) Statement A and B are correct.
(d) Neither Statement A nor Statement B is correct.

31. Which of the following is not a correct table manner?
    (a) Use a napkin
    (b) Sit nicely
    (c) Chew with closed mouth
    (d) Put elbows on the table

32. Which of the following is lighter than ![feather]?

    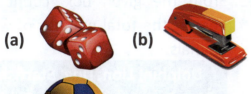
    (a)   (b)

    (c)   (d) None of these

33. What is descending order of 15, 18, 20, 13, and 17?
    (a) 20, 18, 17, 15, 13
    (b) 13, 15, 17, 18, 20
    (c) 15, 13, 18, 17, 20
    (d) 20, 17, 18, 15, 13

34. To which sport is Mary Kom related?

    (a) Badminton (b) Tennis
    (c) Boxing   (d) Hockey

35. In which sport are the equipment shown in the picture used?

    (a) Hockey   (b) Cricket
    (c) Skating (d) Football

36. Which of the following is the brain of computer?

    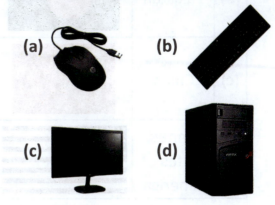

37. Earth gets its light from _____.
    (a) Moon   (b) Sun
    (c) Venus   (d) Neptune

Direction: Read the following clues and complete the given word puzzle for questions 38-40.

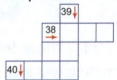

38. The word that rhymes with 'Band'.
    (a) Sand   (b) Tape
    (c) Lamp   (d) Bend

39. A _____ of cards.
    (a) Herd   (b) Pack
    (c) Banana (d) Flock

40. The word that goes with 'Note'.
    (a) Book   (b) Hook
    (c) Fly   (d) Splash

41. Identify the incorrect match.

	Column I	Column II
(a)	India	🇮🇳

General Knowledge One For All Olympiads Solved Papers, Class-1

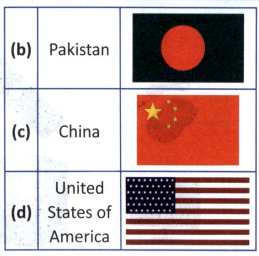

(b)	Pakistan	
(c)	China	
(d)	United States of America	

42. _____ have consciousness.
 (a) Humans
 (b) Machines
 (c) Both (a) and (b)
 (d) Neither (a) nor (b)

43. Reema has 4 candies. Hritik has 7 candies. How many in all?
 (a) 12 (b) 11
 (c) 10 (d) 47

44. 20 − _ = 20
 (a) 1 (b) 2
 (c) 0 (d) 10

45. From the given box, count and answer the total number of water animals.

Dolphin, Lion, Dog, Starfish, Cow, Sparrow, Octopus, Rabbit, Ostrich

 (a) 1 (b) 2
 (c) 3 (d) 4

ACHIEVERS SECTION

1. Which of the following on unscrambling will give the name of a state of India?
 BJUNAP
 (a) Puran
 (b) Punjab
 (c) Bihar
 (d) Bijnaur

2. Rani has a note of ₹ 200. She wants to buy two items. She can buy_____ and _____.
 1. ₹ 50
 2. ₹ 150
 3. ₹ 80
 4. ₹ 120

 (a) Ball and Teddy Bear
 (b) Teddy Bear and Car
 (c) Teddy Bear and Chips
 (d) Ball and Car

3. I have a little nose,
 I have a little chin,
 I have a little _____,
 Just to put my dinner in.
 (a) Mouth (b) Eyes
 (c) Ears (d) Hands

Sample Question Paper, Level-2

4. Match the following.

	Column I		Column II
A.	Eyes	1.	(walking figure)
B.	Legs	2.	(megaphone)
C.	Ears	3.	(ice cream)
D.	Tongue	4.	(television)

(a) A-4, B-1, C-3, D-2
(b) A-4, B-1, C-2, D-3
(c) A-4, B-2, C-1, D-3
(d) A-1, B-4, C-2, D-3

5. Which of the following is odd one?
(a) Virat Kohli
(b) Milkha Singh
(c) Sania Mirza
(d) Lionel Messi

Answer-Key

LEVEL 1

1. (b)	2. (a)	3. (c)	4. (b)	5. (d)
6. (a)	7. (a)	8. (d)	9. (d)	10. (b)
11. (a)	12. (a)	13. (c)	14. (c)	15. (d)
16. (b)	17. (a)	18. (a)	19. (a)	20. (c)
21. (a)	22. (c)	23. (c)	24. (b)	25. (a)
26. (a)	27. (b)	28. (b)	29. (b)	30. (b)
31. (d)	32. (d)	33. (a)	34. (c)	35. (a)
36. (d)	37. (b)	38. (a)	39. (b)	40. (a)
41. (b)	42. (a)	43. (b)	44. (c)	45. (c)

ACHIEVERS SECTION

1. (b)	2. (a)	3. (a)	4. (b)	5. (d)

Answers with Explanations

LEVEL 1

1. **Correct option is (b)**

   Explanation:
   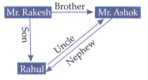

2. **Correct option is (a)**

   Explanation: Akshay, Ravi and Amita are siblings.

3. **Correct option is (c)**

   Explanation: Skin gives us the feel of touch.

4. **Correct option is (b)**

   Explanation: Nurse helps doctor to take care of patients and also helps people when they are sick and hurt.

5. **Correct option is (d)**

   Explanation: Shoulder is one of our body parts that helps us to twist our arms.

6. **Correct option is (a)**

   Explanation: Root grows inside the soil and supports the plant by holding the plant firmly in its place.

7. **Correct option is (a)**

   Explanation: Tulsi is a herb. Banyan is a tree. Pumpkin is a creeper. Money plant is a climber.

8. **Correct option is (d)**

   Explanation: Cow is a domestic animal and Peacock is a bird.

9. **Correct option is (d)**

   Explanation: Roots are buried inside the soil which hold plants firmly at their place.

10. **Correct option is (b)**

    Explanation: Leaf is a green part of plant where the food is made for plant and this food is transferred to various parts of plants through stem. Flower is a reproductive structure of plant that changes into a fruit. Seeds are found inside the fruit.

11. **Correct option is (a)**

    Explanation: Climbers are plants which grow vertically with the help of other plants or objects. Papaya is an example of fruit.

12. **Correct option is (a)**

    Explanation: Monkey, Horse, Lion, Sheep

13. **Correct option is (c)**

    Explanation: Taj Mahal is located in Agra which was built by the great Mughal emperor Shah Jahan. It is one of the seven wonders of the world.

14. **Correct option is (c)**

    Explanation: People prepare seviyan on Eid.

15. Correct option is (d)

Explanation:

Independence Day	15th August	India got independence.
Republic Day	26th January	Constitution of India came into force.
Teacher's Day	5th September	Birth anniversary of great teacher and scholar, Dr. Sarvepalli Radhakrishnan.
Children's Day	14th November	Birth anniversary of Pt. Jawaharlal Nehru who advocated for education of children.

17. Correct option is (a)

Explanation: Except table all are examples of machines.

18. Correct option is (a)

Explanation: Volley ball is played between two teams having six players on each side who are separated by a net.

19. Correct option is (a)

Explanation: The lowest number that a dice have is 1.

22. Correct option is (c)

Explanation: Following pattern will repeat:

23. Correct option is (a)

Explanation: As per the given calendar, the data which fall on friday are 7, 14, 21, 28.

24. Correct option is (b)

Explanation:

Position	From the left	From the right
1st	Maria	Xiao
2nd	Shaka	Candy
3rd	Hana	Hana
4th	Candy	Shaka
5th	Xiao	Maria

27. Correct option is (b)

Explanation:

Ramnath Kovind	President of India
Rajnath Singh	Defence Minister of India
Narendra Modi	Prime Minister of India
Nirmala Sitharaman	Finance Minister of India

28. Correct option is (b)

Explanation: Chandrayaan-2 is the second mission of India to Moon, launched on 22nd July 2019, by the Indian Space Research Organisation, after Chandrayaan-1.

29. Correct option is (b)

Explanation:

Sorry	It is said to apologize.
Thank you	It is said to show gratitude.

| Welcome | It is said in response to thank you. |
| Please | It is said when to ask for something. |

30. Correct option is (b)

Explanation: We should not push others to go ahead.

31. Correct option is (d)

Explanation: We should not rest our elbows on the table while eating as it is incredibly bad for our digestion.

32. Correct option is (d)

Explanation: The feather is lightest among all.

33. Correct option is (a)

Explanation: Descending order is the arrangement of numbers from largest to smallest.

34. Correct option is (c)

Explanation: Mary Kom is an Indian boxer.

36. Correct option is (d)

Explanation: CPU is called 'Brain of the Computer' as it stores all the information.

37. Correct option is (b)

Explanation: Plants don't have their own light. They all shine with the light of the Sun.

38. Correct option is (d)

Explanation: 'Band' and 'Sand' are rhyming words as they are ending with an identical sound.

39. Correct option is (b)

Explanation: Pack is a collective word used for cards, dogs, hyenas, lies, wolves, and hounds.

40. Correct option is (a)

Explanation: Notebook is a single word which means a book for writing notes.

41. Correct option is (b)

Explanation:

| Flag of Pakistan |  |

42. Correct option is (a)

Explanation: Humans have consciousness as they have ability to understand the situation and behave accordingly.

43. Correct option is (b)

Explanation: 4 + 7 = 11

| | | | + | | | | | | | = | | | | | | | | | | |

44. Correct option is (c)

Explanation: If you subtract 0 from any number, you get the same number.

45. Correct option is (c)

Explanation: Water Animals: Dolphin, Starfish, and Octopus

ACHIEVERS SECTION

1. **Correct option is (b)**
   Explanation: Punjab is a state in northern India.

2. **Correct option is (a)**
   Explanation: 150 + 50 = 200

3. **Correct option is (a)**
   Explanation: Mouth is a part of digestive system which is used to chew the food.

4. **Correct option is (b)**
   Explanation: Eyes are used to watch television. Legs are used to walk. Ears are used to hear sound of speaker. Tongue is used to taste ice-cream.

5. **Correct option is (d)**
   Explanation: Lionel Messi is not an Indian player.

General Knowledge One For All Olympiads Solved Papers, Class-1

Exclusive School Books Suppliers

HYDERABAD	**TELANGANA** Sri Balaji Book Depot, 9676996199, (040) 27613300
GUNTUR	**ANDHRA PRADESH** Y Renuka Devi, 9490450750
TEZPUR	**ASSAM** Dutta Book Stall, 9402477623, 8729948473
JAMNAGAR	**GUJARAT** Vidyarthi Book Centre (S.S.D.), 9879014367
RAJKOT	Royal Stationery, 9824207514
TUMKUR	**KARNATAKA** Palasandra Promoters, 9448214377, (0816) 2273220
SALEM	**TAMIL NADU** Salem Book House, 9443324584, (0427) 2411315
PANCHKULA	**HARYANA** Raghubar Dass Sat Prakash, 8950055303
INDORE	**MADHYA PRADESH** Raghav Pustak Sadan (S.S.D.), 7772988088

OUR DISTRIBUTORS

GUNTUR	**ANDHRA PRADESH** Y Renuka Devi, (0863) 2252308, 9490450750
HYDERABAD	Sri Balaji Book Depot, (040) 27613300, 9866355473
VIJAYAWADA	Sri Kanaka Durga Book Stall, 9603491009, 9849144007
	Akshaya Books Corner, 9666155555
VISAKHAPATNAM	Sri Rajeshwari Book Link, (0891) 6661718, 9848036014
GUWAHATI	**ASSAM** Ashok Publication, 7002846982, Book Emporium, 9675972993, 6000763186
	Kayaan Enterprises, (0361) 2630443, BLJ Publications, 7086099332
TINSUKIA	C. R. Book House, 9957886562
PORT BLAIR	**ANDAMAN** Krishna Book Centre, 9474205570
MUZAFFARPUR	**BIHAR** Pustak Bhandar, 9097046555
JHANJHARPUR	Krishna Book Agency, 9801019292, 9304977755
PATNA	Bokaro Student Friends, (0612) 2300600, 2618400, Gyan Ganga Ltd., 9304826651
	Nova Publisher & Distributors, (0612) 2666404,
	Sharda Pustak Bhandar, 8877279953, Shri Durga Pustak Mandir, 9334477386
	Vikas Book Depot, (0612) 2304753, 7004301983
PURNIA	Chaurasia Book Centre, 9006717044, 7004456102
RAIPUR	**CHATTISGARH** Agarwal Traders & Pub., (0771) 4044423, 7489991679, 8878568055 (W. app)
	Gupta Pustak Mandir, 9329100851
DURG	Bhagwati Bhawani Book Depot, 7882327620, 9827473100
DELHI	**DELHI** Mittal Books, (011) 23288887, 9899037390
	Bokaro,Student Friends Pvt Ltd., 7004074400
	R. D. Chawla & Sons, 9899445522, Zombozone, 9871274082
	Sharda Publication, 9971603248
NOIDA	Prozo (Global Edu4 Share Pvt. Ltd), 9899037390, 8587837835, 9318395520
	Global Islamic Publication, 9873690828
AHMEDABAD	**GUJARAT** Patel Book, 9898184248, 9824386112, 9825900335
	Shalibhadra Stationers, 9904477855
VADODARA	Pooja Book Shop, 7600817198, (0265) 2280464
	Umakant Book Sellers & Stationery, 9824014209, 9624920709
VAPI	Goutam Book Sellers, 9081790813
NAVSARI	College Store, 8141913750
BOKARO	**JHARKHAND** Bokaro Student Friends, (0654) 2233094, 7360021503
	Sahu Pustak Bhandar, 9431378296, 7979845480
DHANBAD	Bokaro Student Friends, (0326) 3590527
RANCHI	Bokaro Student Friends, 9234628152, Gyan Ganga Ltd., 9117889900
BENGALURU	**KARNATAKA** Sri Sai Ram Book traders, 9738881088
	Sapna Book House, (080) 46551999, 9343366670
BANGLORE	Hema Book House, 80414851110
GULBARGA	L.E. Bhavikatti, (08472) 261400, 9880737400
HUBLI	Renuka Book Distributor, (0836) 2244124
BELLARY	Chaitanya Exhibition, Bellary - 9886393971
ERNAKULAM	**KERALA** Asad Book Centre, (0484) 2370431, 9447314548, Academic Book House, (0484) 2376613
	Surya Book House, (0484) 2363721, 9847124217, Surya Book Centre, (0484) 2365149
	Orbit Book Centre, 9847770749
KADAVANTHRA	H & C Stores, (0484) 2203683, 2204683, 9446411997
JOMES SRINILAYAM	H & C Store, (0484) 2351233
KOLLAM	H & C Store, (0474) 2765421, 9447574778, H & C Store-2, 9995214104, 9809002519
KOTTAYAM	H & C Store, (0481) 2304351, Book Centre, (0481) 2566992
PALARIVATTOM	H & C Store, (0484) 2344377
TRIVANDRUM	Academic Book House, (0471) 2333349, 9447063349,
	H & C Store, (0471) 2572010, 9446411996
	Engineers Book Centre, (0471) 2596959
KANNUR	Athulya Books, (0497) 2709294
CALICUT	Aman Book Stall, (0495) 2721282,
MORENA	**MADHYA PRADESH** Shri Ram Book Store, 9424603124
GWALIOR	Agarwal Book Depot, 9425116210
INDORE	Student Book Depot, (0731) 2503333, 2535892, 9425322330
REWA	Arun Prakashan, (0731) 2459448, 9424890785
	Siddharth Enterprises, 9425185072
JABALPUR	Sangam General Store, (0761) 2412592, Akash Book Distributor, 9974264828
	New Radhika Book Palace, 9425411533-66
MARGO	**GOA** Golden Heart Emporium, (0832) 2725208, 9370273479
ROHTAK	**HARYANA** Swami Kitab Ghar, 9255121948
GURGAON	Pahuja & Co., 9999563778
SOLAN	**HIMACHAL PRADESH** Mangla Enterprises, 9882050720
IMPHAL	**MANIPUR** Jain Book Shop, 9856031157
JALGAON	**MAHARASHTRA** Sharma Book Depot, 9421393040
KOLHAPUR	**MAHARASHTRA** Ashish Book Depot, 7798420420, Jai Book Co., 9422046679
PUNE	Sai Shubham, 9975687677, (020) 69498635,
	Goel Mini Market, 9890825884, 9028943031,
	Praveen Sales, 9890683475
	Vardhaman Educational, 9834678521
JALNA	Anil Paper Mart, 9422722522, (02482) 230733
WARDHA	Unique Traders, (07152) 243617, 8600044411, 9960644752
IMPHAL	**MANIPUR** Jain Book Shop, 9856031157
KARWI	Ramji & Sons, 9026303241
KOLKATA	**WEST BENGAL** Eureka book Emporium, (033) 25934001, 9433089132
	Schoolwale & Company, 9731715655
MIRZAPUR	**UTTAR PRADESH** Pustak Bhawan, 9936500469
AGRA	Maheshwari Pustak Bhandar, 9760602503
MUMBAI	Shivam Books & Stationery, (022) 28230897, 9892935799
	Student Book Depot, 9821550165
NAVI MUMBAI	Krishna Book Store, (022) 27744962, 9819537938
NANDED	Abhang Pustakalaya, 9823470756
NASHIK	Rahul Book Centre, (0253) 2599608, 9970049681
NAGPUR	Laxmi Pustakalay Stationers, (0712) 2727354, Novelty Book Depot, 9657690200
	Renuka Book Distributor, 9765986633.
	Karamveer Book Depot, 9923966466, 7172725726
	Vijay Book Depot, 9860120094, (0712) 2520496, 2534217
	Shree Mahalaxmi Pustakalaya, (0712) 2283580, 7507099360
PUNE	Natraj Book Depot., (020) 24485054, 9890054092
	Vikas Book House, 9860286472, (020) 244683737
	Mahesh Book & General Store, 9421036171, Kirti Book Agnecies, 9881190907
YAVATMAL	Dilip Book Agency, (0823) 2245450, 9423131275
SOLAPUR	Jitesh Vastu Bhandar (0217) 2741061, 9960000009
DHULE	Navjeevan Book Stall, 7020525561
BHUSAWAL	Anil Book Depot, 9403942906
CUTTACK	**ODISHA** A. K. Mishra Agencies, 9437025991, 9437081319
BHUBANESHWAR	M/s Pragnya, 8847888616, 9437943777, Bharati Book House, 9438420527
BARIPADA	Trimurthi Book World, (0679) 2253336 9437034735
LUDHIANA	**PUNJAB** Amit Book Depot., 9815807871, Ravi Book Shop, 9815200925
	Bhatia Book Centre, 9815277131, 7901814043
JALANDHAR	Cheap Book Store, 9872223458, 9878258592, Gaurav Book, 9478821183
	Subhash Book Depot, 9876453625, Cheap Book Store, 9872223458
	City Book Shop, 9417440753
PATIALA	Adarsh Enterprises, 9814347613
BARNALA	Navchetan Book Depot, 9779050692
BHATINDA	Bhagwati Book, 9463120564, Agarwal Book, 9417816439
SANGRUR	Jindal Book Depot, 9876141679
KOTA	**RAJASTHAN** Raj Traders, (0744) 2429090, 9309232829, 8005529594, Bhandari Stationers, (0744) 231958, Radhe Traders, 8769802001, Perfect Stationers & Gen. Shoppe, 9829863904
BHILWARA	Nakoda Book Depot, (01482) 243653, 9214983594
JAIPUR	J K Enterprises, 9460983939, 9414782130, Education Point, 9269664791
	Saraswati Book House, (0141) 2610823, 9829811155
	Ravi Entreprises (0141) 2602517, 9828944479
	Manohar Book Distrubutor, 9414072321
COIMBATORE	**TAMIL NADU** Majestic Book House, (0422) 2384333
	CBSE Book Shop, (0422) 2303533, 8056655337
CHENNAI	Arraba Book Traders, (044) 25387868, 9841459105, Mr Book Store (044) 25364596, Indian Book House, (044) 24327784, 9094129595,
	Kalaimagal Store, (044) 5544072, 9940619404, Vijaya Stores, 9381037417
	Ruby Books, (044) 26425958, 9884519471, Kamal Store. 9840276067
	Bookmark It-Books & Stat. Store, 7305151653, M.K. Store, 9840030099
	Tiger Books Pvt. Ltd., 9710447000, M. K. Store, 9840030099
PUDUCHERRY	Sri Saraswathi Book Stall, (04132) 222283, 9092626287
TRICHY	Trichy Book House, (0431) 2764198, 2766815, 9489764192. 9443238419
OOTY	Bharat & Co., 9095552155
AGARTALA	**TRIPURA** Book Corner, 9856358594, Book Emporium, (0381) 2391509, 9436460399,
AGRA	**UTTAR PRADESH** Ajay Book Depot, (0562) 2254621, 9411205449
	K. S. A. Book Distributor, 9149081912
	Om Pustak Mandir, (0562) 2464014, 9319117771,
	Panchsheel Books, 9412257961, 9412257962,
ALIGARH	Shaligram Agencies (0571) 2421887, 9412317800
ALLAHABAD	Mehrotra, (0532) 2266865, 9415636890
AZAMGARH	Sasta Sahitya Sadan, 9450029674
BALIA	Vidya Kendra, 9415281234
FARRUKHABAD	Anurag Book, (0569) 2226843, 9839933650
GORAKHPUR	Central Book House, 9935454590
JAUNPUR	Thakur Pustak, 9795198974, 5453-222298
LUCKNOW	Rama Book Depot, (0522) 4080133, 9956922433 (Retail), Vyapar Sadan, 7607102462
MORENA	Shri Ram Book Store, 9424603124
MEERUT	Ideal Book Depot, (0121) 4059252, 9837066307
	Garg Book Depot, 9927052149
VARANASI	Bokaro Student Friends, (0542) 2401250, 8299344607
	Gupta Books, 9918155500, 8707225564
	Shri Krishna Book & Stationery, 9415020103
KOLKATA	**WEST BENGAL** Eureka Book, (033) 25934001, 9433089132, Oriental Publishers & Distributor (033) 40628367, Katha 'O' Kahani, (033) 22196313, 22419071,
	Saha Book House, (033) 22193671, 9333416484,
	New National Book Store, 8697601392,
	United Book House, 9231692641, (033) 22418105
ASANSOL	Book House, 9434747506
SILIGURI	Agarwal Book House, (0353) 2535274, 9832038727, Metro Books, 9832477841